Organize *for* Disaster

PREPARE YOUR FAMILY AND YOUR HOME FOR ANY NATURAL OR UNNATURAL DISASTER

Judith Kolberg

Published by
Squall Press
P.O. Box 691
Decatur, GA 30031

"Individual Preparedness and Response to Chemical, Radiological, Nuclear, and Biological Terrorist Attacks: A Quick Guide," Lynn E. Davis, et al., MR-1731/1-SF, Santa Monica, CA: RAND Corporation, 2003. Pages 3, 7, 11, 15, 21 and 23. Reprinted with permission.

2nd printing 2007
Printed in the United States

Library of Congress Catalog Card Number: 2004096901

ISBN: 0-9667970-4-3

Book and cover design by Jill Dible
Cover photography courtesy of FEMA
Illustrations by Steve Sweny

This book is dedicated to my Dad, Leonard Kolberg,
my Aunt Irene and my Uncle Harry

TABLE OF CONTENTS

TABLE OF CONTENTS (cont.)

ACKNOWLEDGMENTS

This book could not have been possible without the generous interview time and expertise contributed by individuals from FEMA, GEMA, the Salvation Army, and other agencies, in addition to individuals such as Jeff Jellets, Dr. William L. Waugh, Jr., Bill McNutt, Lynne Keating, Ann Lamb, Phillip Webber, Jone Scott, Ken Burris, and Glenn Allen.

In addition, the people who experienced disaster firsthand, including many of my colleagues in the organizing profession, deserve mention for adding their unique stories and perspective to the book. Those people include Sheri Lynch, Donna Cowan, Deena McClain and Ronald McClain, Elizabeth Moss, Lynda Turner, Cyndi Seidler, Vicky Dehnert, Nanci McGraw, Roxy Hambleton, Barbara Summer, Elaine Sexton, Margaret Murray, Frances Strassman, Pam Condie, Sonia Rebollo-McCloskey, and Linda Richards.

I would like to acknowledge individuals who lent their specialized knowledge to the book, including Harvey Horowitz, Bob Hejl, Vic Rachael, Ron Alford, Solomon Green II, Jena Blackshear, Rick Bell, John West, and Amy Fitzgerald.

Naomi Kolberg, Elaine Cohen, and Kim Cossette provided research support, so critical to a book of this kind.

A book is only as good as its editing, and I would like to thank Zebra Communications and Debbie Stanley for their great editing. The book has a powerful cover and a beautiful interior because of the expertise of Jill Dible, who has the added virtue of being very patient. Trusty Stephen Sweny has come through (again) with great illustrations.

My deepest appreciation goes to Sue Williams, who is providing key promotional support for the book and has proven to be a great assistant. A special thanks to Linda McGuire and my mom, Eleanor Kolberg, who stood by me every step of this long endeavor.

PREFACE

Americans were targeted for a terrorist attack on September 11, 2001, for very complex reasons, and the response to that attack is likewise complex, including military, political, and economic decisions that have and no doubt will continue to change our lives. Each of us also had an individual response to September 11. Writing this book is part of my response. Like everyone else, I too wondered, "What can I do?" I know a book about disaster preparedness cannot prevent terrorism or natural disasters, but I also know that being prepared and organized helps tremendously during times of crisis and confusion. When you're organized for disaster you can think more clearly, act with more conviction, and feel safer. I know this from my own clients.

As a professional organizer with fifteen years of experience, I've helped businesses and individuals organize their offices, documents, possessions and homes. My clients have shared with me their commitment to not ever being a grim statistic of disaster, if they can possibly help it. I interviewed professional organizers all over the country, and their stories were the same. People want help organizing themselves, their families, and their homes to cope with disaster. I interviewed disaster experts and obtained even more advice. In all, I interviewed more than sixty individuals. I also reviewed information from the American Red Cross, the Federal Emergency Management Agency, and the Department of Homeland Security. This book combines my knowledge about organization, my interviewing skill, and my writing ability to reach a simple goal: save one person's life. Maybe that person will be you or someone you love.

—Judith Kolberg

INTRODUCTION

Preparing for disaster could save your life and the lives of your family. A survey conducted in 2004 by the American Red Cross and Wirthlin Worldwide (a market research firm) indicates that sixty-seven percent of all Americans agree that it is "very important" to take steps to prepare for a catastrophic event. While awareness is at an all-time high, the same survey revealed that only two in ten Americans feel "very prepared" for a catastrophic event. Only ten percent of American households have a family emergency plan, a disaster kit, and training in first aid and CPR. "It's as if we've recruited a secret army and they haven't gotten their orders…in fact the troops don't even know they are expected to serve," commented American Red Cross President and CEO Marsha J. Evans.

What accounts for this gap between awareness and implementation? Two things: instruction and organization. People know that being prepared for disaster is necessary, but they don't know the exact instructions to follow to effectuate preparedness. They think, "I'm convinced I must get prepared, but what exactly should be my next steps?" Even with precise instructions, many people are not organized enough to implement instructions. They think, "I know I need to see if all my flashlights have working batteries and I've got to buy some bottled water, but where will I find the time?"

Organize For Disaster: Prepare Your Family and Your Home for Any Natural or Unnatural Disaster closes the gap between awareness and implementation. It answers the question of what instructions to follow and how to easily and efficiently get organized and prepared for any disaster. This book contains organizing tools to help you to get prepared right now, so you won't put it off. You'll learn what disaster provisions to have on hand, and you'll have actual shopping lists to make purchasing them simple. You'll know what provisions to store away, and you'll have actual storage ideas. You'll know what plans your family needs to write up; and you'll have actual sample plans, forms, and checklists to assist you. Another organizing tool, called 'The Essentials,' is the final chapter of the book. The Essentials is a ready reference to the most crucial disaster preparedness steps, written in priority order. The index to this book is extensive, the table of contents is easy to use, and the resource section provides even more information sources.

Following is a list of the common risks to your family and your home during a disaster. Each risk is addressed in the book with complete instructions and organizing tools to keep you and your family as safe as possible.

Disaster Risks
- Personal injuries
- Damage to your home
- Lack of essential services, especially electrical power and phone service
- Conditions that require you to remain in your home
- Inability to or difficulty in obtaining reliable disaster information
- Delayed access to emergency aid because those more in need receive it first
- Damage or destruction to your possessions, documents, and personal records
- Conditions that necessitate evacuation and/or alternative shelter
- Extreme emergencies requiring rapid escape

"We need to narrow the universe of the unprepared–those we need to worry about in catastrophic situation. Every one of those unprepared Americans is a potential barrier to the effectiveness of our response to disaster," notes Evans. You do not need to be strong or brave or an expert to get organized and be prepared for disasters. Anyone can do it. According to Susan Neely, assistant secretary for Public Affairs at the Office of Homeland Security, mothers are two-thirds more likely than other family members to make preparedness plans, but even children can contribute to family preparedness. Each chapter contains a special section called What Kids Can Do.

When you use the organizing tools in the book, disaster preparedness becomes not an extra-special task to do when the urgency of a crisis motivates you, but instead, an easy-to-manage part of your family's everyday activity. For instance, you can purchase disaster provisions when you do your regular shopping. You can practice a family evacuation any time of the year. You can maintain safety equipment, such as replacing batteries in flashlights, as easily as you would perform any home maintenance.

Everyday preparedness has the added benefit of improving the quality of your life in general. Knowing first aid, for instance, can benefit you or someone you care for, or even a perfect stranger, during a traffic accident or household accident, not only when a major disaster strikes. "When my kids went off to college, I gave them a map with the most direct route home and an alternative route if that route was blocked due to a disaster. Now, whenever there is a traffic jam, they take the 'disaster' route, even though there is no disaster," says Ken Burris, director of Operations, Department of Homeland Security.

In case you thought reading about preparedness would be dull and boring, you'll find an abundance of interesting information in this book to hold your attention and motivate you, like the stories and advice from people who have experienced disaster firsthand and from on-the-ground disaster experts. *Organize for Disaster* also contains disaster preparedness tips from professional organizers all around the country who understand the powerful combination of organization and preparedness. There are also fun facts, too, such as the history of the emergency phone system 911 and the origins of first aid.

LET'S GET STARTED!

CHAPTER ONE

It Could Never Happen to Me

If I Only Knew Then What I Know Now..._Jone Scott has survived a flood, an earthquake, a typhoon, and a tornado, experiences that prompted her to become active with the Salvation Army's disaster services. Being prepared for disasters has become a way of life for her, but it wasn't always that way._

All the spring flowers were in bloom up and down our neighborhood streets, families worked in their yards, kids played and there was not a cloud in the sky. My husband, son, daughter-in-law and grandchildren were at my house preparing dinner and watching the weather warnings on TV. As we watched, the storm front grew larger. The weather map showed a tornado heading straight for our area. In just moments, the worst warning came. 'Get below ground if possible. The tornado is taking everything above ground! If you cannot go underground, go inside a bathroom or closet in the northeast part of your home!'

We went into the bathroom expecting the storm to turn as it always had before. We could hear the noise coming. My sister called, asking if we were okay. I said, 'I don't know yet.' The phone went dead. The lights went out. We could hear the wind ripping wood and breaking glass. Then all went deathly quiet.

We felt in the dark; we were all okay. When it was safe enough, we walked outside. It looked like a bomb had exploded and flattened everything. Some of our neighbors started appearing out of the rubble, dazed with disbelief. As if by an unspoken command, we all started to try to find the neighbors we did not see. We had no electrical power. Nobody could get in and we could not *leave the area. We were cut off from the world outside. In only thirty seconds, a tornado had flattened a whole neighborhood changing many lives forever.*

Never say it will not happen to you. Many people were killed or injured that day and night, some because they did not heed the warnings, others who did not know how to take precautions. It can *happen to you. It is not just about having a disaster kit. All the duct tape and plastic sheeting in the world may not protect you. You have to get organized!* — Jone Scott, Oklahoma Service Unit Representative, Salvation Army

Chances are you won't experience as many natural disasters as Scott has, but her advice is still sound for all of us. Mother Nature will continue to throw us curves. Man-made disasters like nuclear accidents and chemical spills will no doubt recur, and terrorism is, unfortunately, a new reality to contend with. Being prepared for terrorism and man-made disasters, or what might be called "unnatural" disasters, as well as natural disasters requires advance planning.

Getting organized is all about advance planning and preparing *now* for what might go wrong later, *whether it does go wrong or not.* Getting organized is about getting ready for "just-in-case" scenarios. For instance, 60,000 people were evacuated from their homes during the 2003 wildfires in Southern California *just in case.* Ultimately, only 3,400 of those homes burned. Was the precaution of evacuating worth it to those families, especially those whose homes did not catch fire? John Lowe, who experienced the wildfires firsthand would do it all again at a moment's notice.

Nobody really wants to leave his home. Your home is your family's shelter and it contains all your memories. And for a moment I had this fleeting thought . . . is leaving really worth it? What are the chances of my house being burned? Well it *is* really worth it. Why? Because you just don't know if your house is going to burn or not. You just don't know. As it turned out my house is still standing. Am I bitter because I could have stayed? Am I mad because the firefighters got it wrong? No. You have to be prepared to evacuate because it's the right thing, just in case.

Disasters are crises. When they occur they are special events that require specific action. Even though disasters are crises, they are also an inevitable fact of everyday life. If you interpret disasters as inevitable, it makes perfect sense to prepare for them in an everyday way. The problem with waiting until disaster is imminent—if you are even afforded that luxury—has to do with fear. Fear is a normal, natural response to danger; but fear's effect on thinking and action can be deadly. Just when you need clear, quick thinking, your heart rate goes up. Emotions are strong. Adrenaline, a powerful hormone, is released into the body. Your brain can feel overwhelmed.

You've heard all the adages, from the Boy Scout motto "Be prepared" to "Better safe than sorry," and Ben Franklin's "An ounce of prevention is worth a pound of cure." Where disasters are concerned, being prepared in advance is critical. But thinking ahead *now* for a circumstance that may happen later or not at all is counter-intuitive to most of us. We may "get" the logic of thinking ahead, but the urgency of it escapes us, so we don't prepare.

Organization is the key. The more organized and prepared you are beforehand, the fewer details you will have to think through later. The relief from thinking through the details can leave you just enough time and clarity to make life-saving decisions. Jason Fletcher can attest to that.

"We had a plan for getting in touch with each other if the river ever overflowed and the house was affected by a flood. Sure enough, 2004 brings storm after storm to Kansas, and the house nearly floated away. I'll admit I felt pretty panicky. Thank goodness we had a plan. It wasn't perfect because you can't anticipate everything, but it worked."

TYPE OF DISASTERS

According to the combined information on the websites of the Department of Homeland Security (DHS), the American Red Cross (ARC), and the Federal Emergency Management Agency (FEMA), there are more than thirty-five kinds of disasters. They fall into three main categories: natural or weather-related disasters; man-made disasters; and acts of terrorism. Preparing for each kind is similar because the risks and threats

TYPE OF DISASTERS

NATURAL OR WEATHER-RELATED DISASTERS

Hurricanes	Fires
Tornados	Wildfires
Windstorms	Earthquakes
Typhoons	Tsunami
Tropical storms	Volcanic eruptions and lava flows
Winter storms including blizzards	Landslides, mudslides, debris slides
Winter freezes (extreme, prolonged cold temperatures)	Heat waves (extreme, prolonged high temperatures)
Ice Storms	Droughts or emergency water shortages
Hailstorms	Famines
Severe storms (intense lightning and thunder)	Plagues
Floods, including flash floods	

MAN-MADE DISASTERS

Hazardous chemical/hazardous material spills

Air pollution (prolonged exposure to dangerous airborne toxins)

Water pollution

Nuclear power plant failures or accidents

Acts of violence (wars, riots, looting, bomb threats, bombings not classified as terrorism)

Power outages unrelated to weather events

Cyber attacks (criminal but non-terrorists intentional disruption of commerce or other infrastructures via computer technology)

ACTS OF TERRORISM (ALSO KNOWN AS NATIONAL SECURITY EMERGENCIES)
Chemical weapon attacks
Biological weapon attacks
Nuclear and radiological attacks
Assassinations and kidnappings
Cyber attacks (intentional disruption of air traffic control, nuclear power plants, military data, or other infrastructures via computer technology as an act of terrorism)

are the same. For instance, there is a chance someone in your family could be injured from a falling ceiling tile, whether the cause is an earthquake or a bombing. There is a chance that hunkering down in your home with adequate food and water will be your best protection during either a snowstorm or a chemical spill. The power might go out, the phones may go down, and it may be difficult for you to communicate due to an electrical storm or a deliberate act of sabotage to the electrical power grid. "From a disaster preparedness point of view, the differences between a terrorist attack and a hurricane are no greater than the difference between an earthquake and a tornado," observes Jeff Jellets, a territorial disaster services coordinator for the Salvation Army.

PREPARING FOR THE UNKNOWN

How can you possibly prepare for all these types of disaster especially if you don't know when or even what the disaster will be? The "unknown" has been and continues to be a part of what constitutes a disaster. Advances in technology and meteorology notwithstanding, even the effects of recurring natural disasters cannot be fully known. We still don't know the exact landfall time of a hurricane, or whether a tornado will hit your house or the one across the street, even though hurricanes and tornadoes have been tracked for almost a century. The winds can suddenly shift, and a wildfire can move in the exact opposite direction than anticipated. No amount of science can predict it; Mother Nature is unpredictable. What *is* known and what *is* predictable are that there will surely be more hurricanes, tornadoes, and wildfires. The lights will surely go out again, trains will spill chemicals, and campfires will burn out of control. The threat is also present that nuclear power plants may leak radiation.

Terrorism raises the fear of the unknown to new levels; it is part of what makes terrorism so terrorizing. On September 11, 2001, a disaster of mega-proportions occurred. Nearly 3,000 people died, leaving 3,051 children with a dead parent. The fire in the collapsed twin towers of the World Trade Center burned for 99 days. The economic cost to the city of New York is estimated at $105 billion.

Can you ever really prepare for an act of terrorism? Monitoring the threat or timing of acts of terrorism is even more difficult than timing natural disasters, even for the professionals whose job it is to do this every day. Preventing terrorism is a complex social and political problem out of the control of most individuals; but you can take steps to organize yourself, your family, and your home to prepare for terrorism. The key is to be realistic about the threat and risk to your family and to plan accordingly.

DON'T BE A VICTIM

During a disaster, emergency aid is prioritized. In the United States, disaster assistance from local, state, and federal agencies assumes that every individual, family, and community will plan and respond within the limits of existing resources *before* other assistance will need to be made available. Governmental disaster agencies do utilize private and voluntary agencies to assist, such as the American Red Cross; the Salvation Army; and other religious, charitable, and humanitarian organizations. Disasters are primarily handled at the local level, however, by fire, police, and emergency medical and rescue crews commonly known as first-responders. Assistance escalates from there.

Local officials and relief workers will be on the scene after a disaster, but they cannot reach everyone immediately. They prioritize emergency assistance, and allocate it based on need rather than on demand. For instance, putting a stop to looting during a power outage may be high on your priority list, but police may decide routing traffic around downed power lines is a better use of their personnel. You might be hot, scared and tired in a stuck elevator, but as long as you're safe, emergency personnel will likely assist people in more imminent danger first.

In addition to providing direct fire, police, and emergency medical services, some of the services that local disaster agencies may provide are the following:

- Directing traffic for emergency vehicles and evacuees
- Clearing debris
- Supplementing law enforcement
- Coordinating utility companies and private contractors
- Assessing the safety of structures
- Addressing public health concerns like protecting the water and food supply and preventing communicable diseases
- Managing shelters
- Coordinating emergency donations of food, clothing, and other provisions
- Communicating with hospitals, families, morgues, and the media
- Providing for counseling and mental health support

From the point of view of local agencies, "If people are prepared, if they can take care of themselves

I've been in the business for 30 years, from firefighter to fire chief, up to federal government level in disaster preparedness. I've fought single-family house fires and the fires at the World Trade Center, and people ask me, 'What can I do to help?' I tell them, 'Don't become a victim.' The resources it takes to address the emergency needs of even a single victim are enormous. The expectation is that all services should be available to all people at the same time. During a disaster that's just not possible. At my agency we constantly manage expectations and define and redefine priorities. If I could tell people one message it would be, 'Be prepared. Don't be a victim.' That way you can take care of yourself and your family, and our resources can be used for people who cannot take care of themselves."
— *Ken Burris, Director of Operations, Department of Homeland Security*

and their families, first-responders can focus on the injured or the trapped and those who cannot take care of themselves. This is essential, especially if the disaster is large or complex when emergency resources are stretched," notes Jellets.

Local emergency agencies are almost always stretched. One reason is that new levels of readiness are required to respond to terrorism in addition to other man-made disasters and natural disasters. Another stress on agencies is the demand for expenditures on better technology. This new technology is critical for improving inter- and intra-agency coordination, more accurate monitoring, and faster warning systems. Finally, the federal budget that at one time helped subsidize state and local disaster efforts is itself stretched to finance the "war on terrorism" during an unstable economy.

We must do all we can for ourselves first, before relying on the resources of disaster agencies. It is our responsibility to be as low a priority as possible in order for resources to be allocated to those more in need.

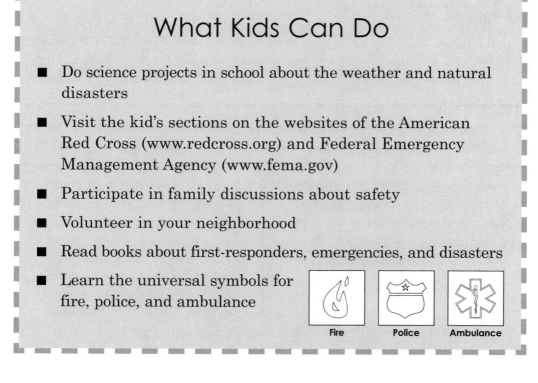

What Kids Can Do

- Do science projects in school about the weather and natural disasters

- Visit the kid's sections on the websites of the American Red Cross (www.redcross.org) and Federal Emergency Management Agency (www.fema.gov)

- Participate in family discussions about safety

- Volunteer in your neighborhood

- Read books about first-responders, emergencies, and disasters

- Learn the universal symbols for fire, police, and ambulance

Fire   Police   Ambulance

CHAPTER TWO

Your Personal Intelligence Network

If I Only Knew Then What I Know Now...*I think the public's view on information is skewed. There is a tendency to think of national news and national leadership as the most credible source. But corroboration is chased down, not up. A single, local building manager and local fire departments are going to know more about what is happening during a fire than state or national sources, even if the incident is large scale. It still happens at a locality. Listen to your local news sources. Determine in advance which ones you think are the most accurate. It may take national intelligence resources to determine whether an incident is caused by terrorism, but its local information that will tell you what action to take. We now understand that all incidents happen locally even if they are spawned internationally. — Burris*

Think about disasters the way the military thinks about "intelligence." You want as much information about your enemy as possible. What is your enemy up to? What will your enemy do next? How will you protect yourself?

Of course, no matter how brutal Mother Nature can seem, she is never really our enemy, but you still must anticipate as much as you can about the havoc that natural disasters can render on you and your family. Unlike Mother Nature, terrorists really *do* mean to inflict harm. The National Weather Service has been tracking hurricanes since 1870, and a very sophisticated early warning system has been developed. Tracking terrorism, however, involves a very complicated intelligence-gathering process that does not afford as clear an early warning system to the public—at least not yet.

Patrick McFadden, Executive Director of the York County (Pennsylvania) Emergency Management Agency said, at a conference of disaster officials, that even under the best of circumstances, it is extremely difficult to alert everyone quickly about an impending threat. Emergency management officials admit that even using every alert system at their disposal, they can reach, at most, only 40% of the people in their jurisdiction within 15 minutes during a daytime disaster.

Disaster agencies work very hard to convey information as a disaster is occurring, as well as warning you before it strikes. They realize that information is essential for quick actions and decision-making. "People want to be *doing* something. They want to act on the information they receive," notes Ann Lamb, Director of Emergency Management in Mitchell County, Georgia, and herself, a disaster survivor. Information delivered promptly and accurately, even if it is sparse, is better than no information at all.

Arthur Moore concurs. Moore was in Manhattan when the Great Blackout of 2003 struck as he was trying to get to his home on Long Island.

"I realize it's hard for emergency workers to communicate what's going on, especially if they don't know any details, but people need information. If I knew the trains and busses wouldn't be running for several hours, I'd be picking out a nice comfortable spot in the park to sleep rather than spinning my wheels trying to figure out how to get home. I'd tell those emergency workers, 'Get on the bullhorns. Tell us the bad news. Tell us the good news. Just tell us the news!'

Disaster officials are up against many obstacles when it comes to disseminating information about disasters. *Warning fatigue* is the term that disaster management officials use to describe the tendency for the public to ignore alerts. This kind of de-sensitivity is something Floridians and Californians know a great deal about.

According to Dr. William Waugh, Jr., a terrorism expert and the author of *Living with Hazards,*

I grew up in southwest Florida and spent my entire life watching hurricane warnings come and go. We became so used to them not amounting to much, that when Hurricane Andrew was due to come, those around me did not take it too seriously. Friends were even throwing hurricane parties and trading stories about wasted time preparing for other hurricanes that never amounted to anything. If you could have seen the destruction Hurricane Andrew brought to southwest Florida, you would know how very foolish it was not to prepare as we should have. —*Jone Scott*

Dealing with Disaster, one reason that people tend to ignore alarms is that they are too busy to respond. They don't want to be distracted from what they are doing by having to figure out what this alarm or that alert means. Another reason, notes Waugh, is, "Unfortunately, people have learned to be suspicious of government officials. They may not fully trust what a government official says."

Difficulties that disaster management officials confront when communicating information include the following:

- Warning fatigue
- Dependence on alternating current (electricity) that often goes down during disasters
- Call blocking, unlisted numbers, fax lines, and internet lines that make telephone communication difficult
- Complexity and incompatibility of interagency high and low technologies including phone, fax, internet, radio channels, satellite feeds, and couriers
- Reliance on cell phones instead of landline phones. Cells phone are less reliable than landline phones.

Given the difficulties that disaster agencies confront, you would be wise to establish your own "intelligence network" made from a combination of the following:

- Traditional warning systems
- Your local social network
- The latest communication technology

TRADITIONAL WARNING SYSTEMS

Your local radio and television stations broadcast "watches" and "warnings." The terms sound so similar that confusion often results. A "watch" sounds like a weather event that has actually been sighted—you can literally "watch" for, but in fact, a watch means that conditions are conducive for a natural disaster such as strong, sustained winds that could result in a tornado, or rising river waters that could produce a flood. A "warning" is more urgent than a watch. A warning means a disaster is imminent, such as a tornado that has touched down or a river that is overflowing.

Here's a way to remember the difference between a watch and a warning. Imagine yourself first checking your wristwatch. Imagine your wristwatch has an alarm. First you check your wristwatch, then you respond to the warning— the alarm—that goes off.

Typically, a watch will precede a warning, but not always. Occasionally a storm appears so suddenly that there is only time for a warning. Listen carefully to radio or TV, and heed the watches and warnings.

TIP Jan Limpach, a professional organizer, advises that if you are out of town during a disaster, know what county you are in. Warnings, watches, and other advisories are county specific.

A battery-operated National Oceanic & Atmospheric Administration (NOAA) weather radio and a battery-operated, transistor radio are affordable, easy options for those times when the electricity may be out and your plug-in radio and TV are not working. The NOAA provides a public service called the National Weather Service (NWS). The NWS is a nationwide network of radio stations with 800 transmitters in all 50 states plus Puerto Rico, the U.S. Virgin Islands, and the U.S. Pacific Territories. NWS broadcasts continuous weather information including warnings, watches, forecasts, and other hazard information 24 hours a day via NOAA radios.

During an emergency, the NWS interrupts routine radio programming and sends out a special tone that automatically activates NOAA radios in the listening area. The NOAA system is designed for natural disasters and man-made disasters, but can also be activated for acts of terrorism with information provided by local and state government officials.

The Emergency Alert System (EAS) uses digital technology to distribute messages. It can provide the President of the United States with a means to address the American people in the event of a national emergency. The NWS can also activate the EAS. The digital signal is transmitted automatically to broadcast stations, cable systems, and certain satellite programmers even if those facilities are unattended. The system is periodically tested with the familiar words, "This is a test of the Emergency Alert System...this is only a test..."

Broadcasts from the NOAA weather radio can be annoying. The broadcast repeats over and over again and has a computerized voice with a distinct non-human sound. You'll be tempted to turn it off. "I can see the headlines now: 'Disaster Coordinator Turns Off Radio. Dies in Tornado.' The radio can be annoying but it will save your life so don't turn it off," Jellets says.

While your NOAA radio will keep you posted technically on the disaster, your local radio station will have specific advice, procedures, and directives relevant to your local community. Your local radio station will have on-the-ground information that other radio stations will not have. Keep a battery-operated radio on hand with plenty of batteries. Some people prefer watching a battery-operated TV. "My TV is only a little bit larger than my radio and though the screen is small, I find seeing the journalists and commentators more comforting than just listening to reports on the radio," comments Cyndi Seidler, who has experienced several disasters in her home state of California.

Learn about the types of potential disasters specific to your area of

TIP If you watch TV during a disaster, be cognizant of the fact that the repeated, explicit images can be harmful to young children. The images increase their anxiety, cause nightmares and frighten them. Turn the TV off and listen to the radio instead.

the country. In Georgia, for example, where this book was written, earthquakes are rare, but hurricanes are not uncommon, and coastal areas are prone to floods. The Centers for Disease Control and Prevention is located in metropolitan Atlanta as are various military installations, a major airport, and the world headquarters of a few multi-national corporations. Terrorists would no doubt find these institutions to be attractive targets. Every locale is different. Visit or e-mail—do not phone—your local emergency management office and ask them what disasters your area is prone to. The staffs of local and county emergency management agencies are limited, and this may not be the kind of information the person answering the phone will have at hand. Your state emergency management agency maintains a website where you can also learn much of this information. Go to the FEMA website at www.fema.gov, which links to every state emergency management office. If you don't own a computer, use one at the local public library.

Following are examples of questions to ask when you visit or e-mail:

- What hazardous materials are produced, stored, or transported in this area?
- What potential terrorist targets are there, such as military installations, high profile landmarks, international airports, nuclear power plants, or large hydroelectric dams?
- What very large public gatherings are held in the area?
- What controversial events are held in the area (i.e., world summits, economic conferences, political events)?
- What natural disasters are common in the area, and what are the disaster seasons?
- What warning sirens and alarms are in effect in my community? What does each sound like, and what does each mean?

Watches and warnings for natural disasters tell us of the likelihood of a natural disaster, and supplemented with news, we know the "where" and the "when" of the event. Determining the "where" and the "when" of a terrorist attack is much more difficult. The Homeland Security Advisory System (HSAS), developed after the September 11, 2001 terrorist attacks, was designed to provide a threat level for a terrorist attack but not necessarily the details.

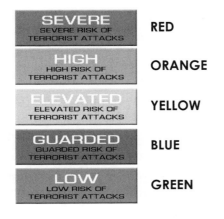

SEVERE SEVERE RISK OF TERRORIST ATTACKS	**RED**
HIGH HIGH RISK OF TERRORIST ATTACKS	**ORANGE**
ELEVATED ELEVATED RISK OF TERRORIST ATTACKS	**YELLOW**
GUARDED GUARDED RISK OF TERRORIST ATTACKS	**BLUE**
LOW LOW RISK OF TERRORIST ATTACKS	**GREEN**

HSAS is meant to inform state and local governments about the status of terrorism threats. It is not designed, strictly speaking, to provide direct, actionable information to individuals or to families. For each level of threat, state and local governments have a well-articulated plan of action that includes specific steps they should take, such as activating crisis communication centers or contacting the FBI. Families and individuals also want to be able to translate the HSAS threat levels into action. They want to know "what do I need to be doing?" because action is a way of being in control, of participating rather than being a passive victim.

Following are suggested actions for families and individuals at each threat level of the HSAS:

Level Green – Develop family communication plan, as well as evacuation and rapid escape plans. Assemble hunker down provisions. Know how to turn off your utilities. Consider taking a first aid course.

Level Blue – In addition to the above, practice all your plans, refresh disaster provisions, regularly consult your personal intelligence network.

Level Yellow – In addition to the above, understand the shelter-in-place plans of your family's schools, daycare, and worksites.

Level Orange – In addition to the above, practice your plans more frequently, and make agree on critical decisions, such as whether to go to work or school or whether to shelter the pets elsewhere.

Level Red - Refrain from attending or being in the presence of targets that may be of interest to terrorists, refrain from traveling unnecessarily, stay calm and informed, follow the instructions of emergency officials.

YOUR LOCAL
SOCIAL NETWORK

"Alerts, warnings, and advisories are not decisive enough and tend not to give enough information. When it comes to the content of information, you cannot give people enough information. People want to take action. The government tends to underinform. When people are underinformed, they will go elsewhere to meet their needs," notes Waugh. To meet their need for information, people consult their local social network, which consists of neighbors, co-workers, friends and family.

Diminished availability of, or access to, disaster-related information *as it is happening* is common. To the credit of the millions of people affected by the Great Blackout of 2003, lack of information did not give way to panic. Part of the reason is that people will turn to their neighbors and find out what they know. Because there were no televisions or computers working, people blasted their car radios—the equivalent of turning to your neighbors, sharing what little information there is. Another example was evidenced during the September 11 attack on the World Trade Center. Coworkers,

bosses, and supervisors—not fire officials—greatly influenced whether or not people on a particular floor were evacuated from the building. (In many instances, though, people simply had no chance to evacuate.)

No one knows whether your local social network will collectively make the right decision, but it is fair to say that your intelligence gathering and decision making is informed not only by what you hear on radio and TV but also by what you learn from people like yourself. People in foreign countries that have experienced terrorism understand the necessity of a local social network. Sonia Rebollo-McCloskey is a 1988 Olympian from Spain. "I believe that what has helped me survive terrorism in Spain since I was very young was to be aware of the news and to be aware of my neighborhood. Be aware of your everyday life, of your neighborhood, but also be aware of political changes in the world and changes that affect your national government," she advises.

Cultivate your local social network in the following ways:

- Get to know your neighbors. Find out who among them can help with a medical emergency or has other skills helpful during disasters.

- Determine together what your families will do to help one another during a disaster.
- Discover who has been through a disaster before and can be relied upon for accurate information and guidance.
- Talk about changes in the world with your friends, family, and neighbors to help you make judgments about your local safety.

USE THE LATEST TECHNOLOGY

The Internet is a remarkable tool for staying informed. Choose a few good websites that deliver real time, accurate information. The website of FEMA at www.fema.gov is excellent. The National Weather Service website at www. weather.gov is also a good choice. The websites of major media companies such as Cable News Network (CNN) at www.cnn.com and the New York Times at www.newyorktimes.com also have a continuous stream of vetted news.

If your computer is down because of a power outage, you can still get on the Internet even if you don't have a battery-powered laptop computer. Desktop computers can perform without electricity when hooked up to an uninterruptible power supply (UPS), also called a battery back-up. Purchase a UPS and you can still access the Internet for crucial disaster information or for communicating by e-mail. Some cell phones now have Internet capability, giving you another option. Internet-based radio is also available, and other technologies are emerging every day that can help you stay informed.

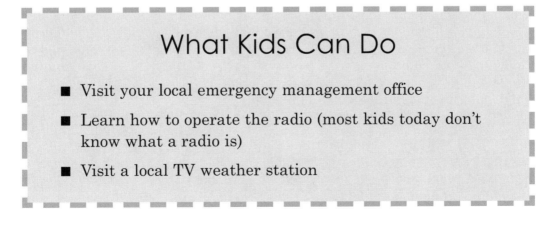

What Kids Can Do

- Visit your local emergency management office
- Learn how to operate the radio (most kids today don't know what a radio is)
- Visit a local TV weather station

CHAPTER THREE

Organize Your Essential and Important Documents

If I Only Knew Then What I Know Now... *"We were lucky. We had a whole day's notice to get ready to evacuate, but instead of spending it with my family helping them pack up, I'm knee deep in the filing cabinets looking for important papers. Is my homeowner's policy under 'House' or 'Homeowners Insurance' or 'Insurance?' I thought, 'I'll need to reach my insurance agent,' but finding her business card was a nightmare. Would I need my birth certificate? I had no idea how to even start finding it. That filing cabinet got organized as soon as they let us return to our homes. And you know what? Most of it was junk!"* — David Ray, Illinois flood evacuee

Organizing your essential and important documents *now* will reward you in the event of a disaster later. These documents enable you to return to the life you had before disaster struck, or to rebuild your life anew. With time and effort, nearly all documents are replaceable from the organization of original issue. There is a chance, however, that the organization of original issue may go out of business or perish in a disaster. "Along with my home, the local courthouse and municipal building were destroyed by the flood. I couldn't get any of my vital records," recalls Warren Hyberg, a victim of a major flood in Indiana.

The Internet has made replacing documents easier than ever before, but it can still be a time-consuming, frustrating process that may impede post-disaster recovery. If you've ever lost your wallet or had it stolen and had to replace the contents, you have a general idea of how exasperating this can be. You do not want to spend your time gathering essential and important papers when disaster strikes.

ESSENTIAL DOCUMENTS

It is likely you will be able to grab your wallet or purse and thus, have some key documents on your person like your driver's license and credit cards. But just in case, it is necessary to put the essential documents listed below in a lightweight, water-resistant container. These essential documents quickly prove your identity, a critical first step in disaster relief. They also allow you to cancel

and replace credit cards. Included in your essential documents are unique, hard-to-replace family papers such as medical records.

- Vital Contact and Vital Codes List (see below)
- Copy of driver's license or other photo identification card
- Original passport
- Copy of Social Security card
- Original citizenship or naturalization papers
- Photocopy of your credit cards (both sides)
- Unique family documents

Choose a container that is lightweight and water-resistant. A good choice is a vacuum-packed bag also called a space bag. Made of layers of polyethylene and nylon these bags seal like food storage bags and

My husband, Nick, was at home when the firestorm broke out. I was in Washington ,D.C., on business when I got Nick's telephone message about the firestorm. Nick said the police told him to pack up the children and evacuate. He was able to get our three young sons in the car. He knew I had our essential papers in a safe place in the house, but I hadn't told him where that was. In the rush to evacuate, he had to leave the papers behind because he simply could not find them. Lesson: Tell your spouse where you put your essential papers.—*Jayne Sorenson, 1991 Oakland firestorm victim*

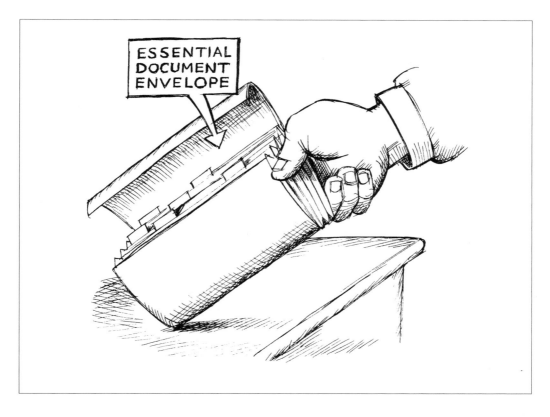

protect against moisture, insects, rodents, mildew, dirt and odor. They also prevent oxidation and decay, and they take up very little space. A plastic, document holder available from an office supply store is also a good option. "I suggest my clients use Doc-U-Keeper (www.docukeeper.com). It's a plastic briefcase with custom-designed pockets already labeled to contain vital documents," offers JoAnn Sheldon, a professional organizer who helps her clients prepare for disaster.

Once you've assembled your essential documents inside a lightweight container, add it to your grab & go bag. The grab & go bag is a backpack kept in a central place in the house along with other disaster provisions. If you do have to evacuate or escape your home rapidly, your essential documents will already be packed and ready to go, along with other critical supplies. For more information about the grab & go bag, see the chapter called Hunker Down.

PROOF OF YOUR IDENTITY

No matter how much you insist that you are who you are, your documents ultimately prove your identity, at least in the eyes of insurance companies, banks, the Internal Revenue Service, governmental agencies, aide organizations, and the myriad of bureaucracies that typify modern life. You will be in contact with many of them if there is a disaster.

"I learned this the hard way," reflects Adrian Moss, a survivor of a huge mudslide in Oregon. "I had nothing on me but the keys to my car. My wallet was on the dresser, but the mudslide was so fast that I just grabbed my pants and my wife's hand and we ran. It was hell starting over. It took over a year to feel like my feet were on the ground again. I felt like I didn't even have an identity."

Essential documents that prove your identity are ones that verify your date of birth, what you look like, the proper spelling of your name, and your official signature.

- **Driver's License or Other Photo Identification Card:** If you don't drive, photo IDs are obtainable wherever driver's licenses are issued and at post offices that issue passports.

- **Birth Certificate:** Agencies require a certified copy with an official governmental seal. This can be obtained from the Department of Vital Records in the county in which you were born. Get one now!

- **Passport:** If you have a driver's license or other photo ID, your passport won't be necessary for identification purposes; however, it is good to have as a backup if you lose your driver's license.

- **Social Security Card:** This is a unique number issued only to you that helps to verify your identity.

UNIQUE INFORMATION ABOUT YOU AND YOUR FAMILY

Every family has unique information about family health or citizenship or other matters. These documents are often difficult to replace and so you may want to include them in your essential documents container.

- medical records (especially if a family member has had extensive therapy, hospitalizations, or rehabilitation)
- immunizations
- citizenship or naturalization papers

VITAL CONTACTS
AND VITAL CODES

In the event of disaster, you would most likely contact your family first. That information is recorded on your Family Communication Plan (see Chapter Seven). The people you will probably want to contact next are called vital contacts. These may include:

- Employer
- Banks, investment institutions
- Credit card companies
- Insurance agents and appraisers
- Power, light, gas, and other utility companies
- Dept. of Motor Vehicles

In addition to vital contacts, you may also want to record personal identification numbers (PINs), passwords, user codes, and other identifiers called Vital Codes. Vital codes are used to log onto your computer, log onto your Internet provider, refill pharmacy prescriptions on-line, pay bills on-line, order merchandise on-line, access financial accounts, use ATMs, turn your security system on and off, lock your cell phone and many other purposes. These vital codes may already be programmed into your computer or you may have them memorized. But it is recommended you write them down. "I was so stressed out by the earthquake, I could hardly remember my name let alone the password to my online IRA account. Then, when I was able to get back on my computer, the data was all scrambled. What a mess. If I had it to do all over again, I would have written the codes down somewhere," notes Bob Harris who has experienced an earthquake firsthand.

Forms you can use to record your vital contacts and vital codes are in the Appendix. Keep the completed Vital Contacts form in your essential document container. If you are concerned that your vital codes might fall into the wrong hands, store that form in your regular filing system, but put a note in your essential document container reminding you to add the form when and if you must evacuate.

IMPORTANT DOCUMENTS

Proof of what you own (money, real estate, the contents of your home, vehicles, etc.) and whom you owe (income taxes, credit cards, loans, etc.) are embodied in important documents of various types. If your property is damaged or destroyed, you'll need proof that you owned it before it can be replaced. You'll want to have documentation of your debts so that you can continue paying them without penalty and maintain your good credit. You may also need these documents to apply for special considerations like tax filing extensions due to disaster hardships. Important documents include:

- Trust records, originals
- Copies of the first two pages of your state and federal income tax returns for the past two years
- Copies of your credit cards (both sides) or the most recent statement from each credit card company
- Deeds, titles, escrow, mortgage notes, or other loan information for real estate
- Stock and bond certificates
- Vehicle titles and registrations including automobiles, motorcy-cles, boats, campers, recreational vehicles, etc.
- Appraisals for rare, collectible, or expensive items such as artwork, antiques, and jewelry

Essential documents are contained for portability. But important documents need to be stored in a safe deposit box off-premises, so if your house is destroyed by a disaster, the important documents will not be damaged. The above important documents will come in handy for dealing with disaster. But you may want to protect other important documents in a bank safe deposit box such as wills and living wills, original power-of-attorney authorizations, and original marriage certificates and divorce decree. Keep an extra key to your bank safe deposit box in your grab & go bag.

There is an off chance that your local bank could be as adversely affected by the same disaster as your home, and you may not have access to your bank safe deposit box. You have several options to deal with this. You can store your safe deposit documents in a bank branch outside your community, or you can mail a copy of the entire set of your safe deposit documents to an out-of-town, trusted friend or family member. Another option is to use a commercial safe deposit box company.

FILING SYSTEMS

All your documents, except for essential documents that go in the grab & go bag, and important documents that go in a safe deposit box, should go into a fire-resistant and water-resistant household filing cabinet, strongbox, or safe, so that they will be well protected. Even if your home is not vulnerable to natural floods, water damage from fire hoses, plumbing problems and other sources of water intrusion is mitigated if the filing cabinet is water-resistant. Be cautious about containers that claim to be fireproof. "We lost everything we owned in the 1991 Oakland, California wildfire. Those 'fireproof' safes for home use are generally totally useless in a really raging fire. Our papers were stored in one and turned to ash," recounts Vicky Dehnert, an organizing consultant living in Oakland at the time. When purchasing a fireproof storage container, look for an Underwriters Laboratory (UL) rating of at least one hour. Be aware that if you plan to store electronic media, such as CDs, in a safe, you'll need a safe with an even higher fire rating.

Clearly mark the file folders inside the filing cabinet on the tab provided. You can either file folders with a simple, alphabetical system using alphabetical dividers, or you can file categorically. For instance, in an alphabetical system, 'Veterinarians' would be filed under V. In a categorical system, Veterinarians would be filed under 'Services' or 'Pet Information'. Keep your categories broad without too many subcategories because subcategories sometimes make documents even more difficult to retrieve.

VIRTUAL SAFE DEPOSIT BOX

Increasing numbers of people are storing their important documents digitally on the Internet. These virtual, or digital, safe deposit boxes afford easy organization, long-term or archival storage, protection, security and ease of use. The drawbacks are several, however:

- The expense for these services
- The possible loss of data due to technological accidents or sabotage

- The need to get to a computer in order to retrieve the documents
- The possibility that the virtual storage company may go out of business

SAFEGUARD BUSINESS RECORDS

An entire body of literature, beyond the scope of this book, is dedicated to protecting business data and to disaster recovery. The most essential information you will need in order to quick-start your business in a post-disaster situation is:

- Client contact information
- Payroll records
- Accounts receivable
- Accounts payable

Download this information regularly to CDs or floppy discs and add the CDs or discs to your essential documents. For more resources on this topic, see the reference section in the back of this book.

TIP E-mail important information to relatives.

PREVENTING IDENTITY THEFT

Unscrupulous people may try to take advantage of you during or after a disaster, including stealing your identity. Documents containing personal information about you can be used to create parallel, fraudulent credit accounts. Criminals use these accounts to purchase goods and services that are then billed to your account. Sometimes you don't know about this criminal activity until months have passed. It is always wise to protect yourself against identity theft. During a disaster, it may be even more important.

Individuals may recover your wallet, checkbooks, investment statements or other documentation left behind in a fire, flood, evacuation, or other disaster event. They may even go through your trash knowing you are preoccupied with other matters. Crooks can use your Social Security card, account numbers, phone card numbers, prescription information and other information to open fraudulent accounts, make unauthorized purchases and ruin your credit. Many of the September 11 terrorists used stolen identification to evade the FBI.

- Shred credit card applications, loan offers and anything with your Social Security Number on it, or start a "burn bag" for burning these materials in your fireplace.
- Order checks *without* your full name, Social Security number, address, or phone number on them. Instead use the initials of your first name and your full last name. Crooks won't know how you sign your name, but your bank will know.
- On checks use a Post Office box instead of an address. Use your work number instead of your home number. Manually add your Social Security number and address only when asked.
- Don't leave personal information in your car.
- Pay with cash whenever possible.
- Don't leave mail with identifiers in the mailbox overnight.

If you suspect you are a victim of identify theft, contact the Federal Trade Commission's Identity Theft Hotline at 1-877-IDTHEFT for up-to-date information on how to work with credit bureaus and law enforcement agencies to reclaim your identity. Also, contact the Social Security-Administration to report misuse of your Social Security number.

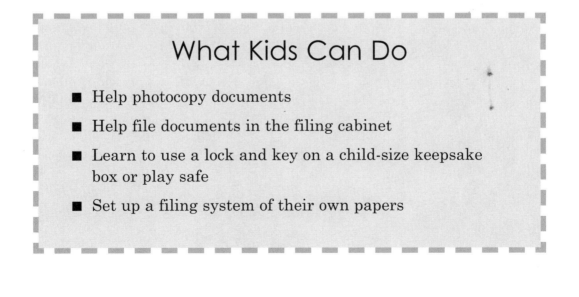

What Kids Can Do

- Help photocopy documents
- Help file documents in the filing cabinet
- Learn to use a lock and key on a child-size keepsake box or play safe
- Set up a filing system of their own papers

CHAPTER FOUR

Insurance Coverage

How to Avoid the Disaster After the Disaster

If I Only Knew Then What I Know Now... *"We hadn't had a tornado in nearly six years. So I guess we all got kind of complacent. Each year, I renewed my homeowner's policy without giving it much thought. Well, the tornado that hit this year took the house with it. Nothing was left standing except the brick fireplace, that's how strong the wind was. But this was our community, where our kids went to school, so we decided to rebuild. The insurance company paid us based on the value of the house when it was built 15 years ago. It's a lot more expensive to build today than 15 years ago. The materials cost more, the labor costs more, and the building codes are different. We paid tens of thousands of dollars out of pocket to cover the gap between our insurance payout and the costs of rebuilding our home. Don't go through that! Read your policy now, before disaster strikes. Sit down with your insurance carrier now. There's always something more you can do to protect yourself from financial disaster!*
— Lou Barnes, tornado survivor, Illinois

HOMEOWNER'S INSURANCE

Many people are under the mistaken impression that the government gives money to people after a disaster to do things like rebuild their homes or replace their possessions. While most state governments do have disaster programs, they are loan-based and not outright money grants. Federal grants are available only if your area is declared by the President of the United States to be a disaster zone. Federal grants are unlikely to be enough to cover the total cost of rebuilding your home after a disaster. Given the limited disaster resources of the state and federal government, homeowner's insurance is very important.

The amount of insurance you buy should be based on the cost to rebuild, not on the market value of your home. The cost to rebuild your home by qualified expert contractors includes their labor, profit, overhead, and materials. The insurance term for the cost to rebuild is "replacement cost." Replacement cost means the insurer will pay the full cost to repair or replace your damaged house with new materials of the like, kind, and quality that was damaged or lost up to the limit of the policy. As many as three-quarters of U.S. homeowners are carrying insurance policies that don't cover replacement costs, according to a study released by the construction firm Marshall & Swift/Boeckh in 2002.

Homeowners tend to believe that the Actual Cash Value (ACV) clauses in their policies will protect them. ACV means the insurer could pay less than the full cost to repair or replace your damaged property. For instance, if you replaced your disaster-damaged roof with a new roof, the insurer is allowed to depreciate or reduce the replacement costs of the new roof based on the age and condition of the original roof. If you want a guarantee that the full cost to rebuild your home will be paid, even if that cost exceeds the limit of your policy, you'll need to purchase guaranteed replacement coverage.

Underinsurance is another problem. A typical policy pays out 120% of the home's assessment value and includes an inflation guard of about two percent annually. But construction and materials costs, however, have increased well over two percent. Another factor increasing the disparity between insurance coverage and replacement cost is renovations. Many Americans renovate their home, increasing its value, but do not increase their insurance coverage. In addition, some homes are in areas where their homes have appreciated but they have not upgraded their insurance to cover the new, appreciated value.

WHAT YOU CAN DO BEFORE DISASTER STRIKES

Make a copy of your insurance policy. Sit down and read it when it is due for renewal. Mark up the copy, underlining parts where you have any questions or don't understand the terms and conditions, exclusions, or limitations. Then call your insurance carrier.

- Be certain your agent's assessment of your home's value is accurate. It should include not only the square footage or number of rooms, but also consideration for the materials used and regional variations in the cost of labor and materials in your geographic area.
- Get a second appraisal from an independent appraiser or ask a local contractor to provide an estimate of what it would cost to rebuild your home.
- Review your policy each time you renovate or make improvements.
- Be sure your policy adequately covers pertinent structures, such as detached garages, fences, in-ground pools, and tennis courts.
- Know how much time you have to file a claim. For instance, damage from earthquakes is not always immediately apparent and you may need to file a claim months from the date of the disaster.
- Make a household inventory to help evidence the losses of personal property (see Chapter Five).
- Be certain your homeowner's policy covers additional living expenses, and temporary repairs and debris removal, which you may incur if your home is badly damaged or destroyed and you must seek shelter elsewhere.

If your home is older, highly renovated, historic or a landmark, try to avoid the "code trap." The code trap is a situation that leaves you underinsured for the cost of bringing your home back up to code if you rebuild after a disaster. Upgrade coverage, also known as ordinance and law coverage, can close the gap, but not every insurance company offers it.

If you have personal property losses due to a disaster, you will be asked by your insurance carrier to submit a Proof of Loss form. Reimbursement for the actual value of the item may not match what you really end up paying to replace the items. That's why you want to be sure your homeowner's policy also calls for replacement cost of personal property.

A household inventory makes the process of proving your personal property losses much easier than attempting to remember them after the fact. See Chapter Five for instructions on how to conduct a household inventory.

Add up all the estimated values on your household inventory to find out the cost to replace everything. Compare this figure to your policy's personal property limit. If there is a gap, purchase more personal property coverage.

Ron Alford, an expert in disaster restoration and property claim recovery, likens adequate insurance to a financial parachute. "You could buy a cheaper parachute and hope nothing disastrous happens. But if disaster happens, is that when you want to find out that your parachute

is missing a few pieces? I think not," he advises.

VALUABLES

Insure your jewelry, silverware and special collections such as coins and stamps. Insurance policies put limits on the value of jewelry, silverware, coins and stamp and other collections, as well as firearms, artwork and collectibles. You may need to purchase a scheduled personal property endorsement, often called a "rider" or a "floater," to cover the additional value of these items. Have your valuables appraised regularly to keep pace with their value.

Keep valuable and infrequently worn jewelry in a bank safe deposit box. A home safe, if it's fireproof and

A woman put on all her expensive jewelry, than trudged on foot in hiking boots and jeans to an emergency shelter! She arrived, bedecked in diamond earrings, pearls, gold necklaces, bracelets and gemstone rings on each finger. Her husband and son had to keep all-night vigils at the shelter to make sure she wasn't mugged. Another woman tossed her wooden jewelry box into the built-in swimming pool in her backyard. It promptly sank to the bottom and stayed there protected from the raging fire that destroyed the house, but it was stolen before the family was able to recover it.

> **TIP** Insure your valuables even if they are inside a bank safe deposit box. The banks do not insure the contents of safe deposit boxes. And pay your bank safe deposit rental fee on time. Depending on which state you live in, the contents can be declared unclaimed property if you fall too far behind in your fees.

waterproof, will also protect your jewelry, but in the event of a disaster, you may not have time to get it open. A safe deposit box is off-premises, so if your home safe is compromised during a disaster, your jewelry will still be protected.

Make certain you have adequate insurance for art, antiques, and collectibles as their appraised value may have increased over the years. Take time to make a thorough, descriptive record of each item, and accompany with individual photographs.

WHAT TO DO
WHEN DISASTER STRIKES

The insurance carrier will want you to notify them immediately, and to protect and preserve your property against further losses. Not doing these two things, gives them an excuse for not honoring your claim. If the insurance carrier does not take your information over the phone,

get the name of someone you spoke with and file a Notice of Loss form; send it by certified mail.

To prevent further losses to your property, immediately turn off the gas, electricity, or water as appropriate. See Chapter Six for instructions on turning off utilities. Then contact qualified emergency services experts who can protect and preserve your property against further loss. Check under "Fire and Damage Restoration" in the Yellow Pages and make sure the expert has credentials from a professional association in their industry. Find an expert who will accept an Authorization and Direct Payment Request in exchange for services. A sample of this form is in the Appendix. This allows them to provide you with services and collect the money from your insurance carrier much like insurance forms used at hospitals.

Disasters can be devastating, not only to your property, but also to your emotions because they can injure or cause the death of people you know and love, or disaster can destroy your home and everything that was once familiar to you. Under these circumstances, managing to call the insurance company or other small steps can be daunting. "Relatives and close friends can be a terrific asset in helping your take control but only if they know you need their help. Contact them and ask for their help," advised Alford.

Friends and family can do the following:

- Witness the damage
- Photograph or videotape the damage
- Provide telephone, office or other facilities
- Run errands for you like faxing and copying
- Store your valuables and important papers
- Lend you things you need
- Provide moral support and humor

DOCUMENT THE DISASTER

It is important to document the disaster itself. This will serve you well for insurance and disaster assistance purposes. Use your friends or family to help you with this task if you are too upset or confused.

- Keep a pocket notebook with you at all times during a disaster. Record the dates of meetings, conversations, or telephone calls with agencies, insurance companies, contractors, relief organizations, and anyone else you are communicating with in order to obtain disaster assistance of any kind.
- Back up any verbal conversations or agreements you have with a fax, letter, or e-mail so that the content of all discussions is documented on paper.
- Keep receipts from emergency service providers as well as for purchases related to evacuation such as lodging, food, and clothing.
- Keep damaged items as material evidence for claiming losses.
- Document damage with a videotape or photographs before repairs are made, even temporary repairs.

The point about keeping receipts cannot be overemphasized. "It cost us $250 to go to the local store just to get the things we needed for bed the night after the fire. Then the next day, we had to go to the store again to buy more basics like underwear and a change of clothes. We couldn't wait for the insurance company to make payments, so I went to our insurance company and got an advance of $5,000 so that we could get by for the next few weeks," recounts Elizabeth Moss, survivor of a California firestorm. A nearby hotel may be a good choice if you are displaced for a week or two, but you may be surprised to know that if you need accommodations for a longer term, a furnished house or apartment might be provided by your insurance carrier.

Unscrupulous individuals can take advantage of you while you are coping with the unfortunate situation of a disaster. Alford has advised many people under these circumstances. He says, "The people who show up at your doorstep the day of a disaster to advocate for or represent your rights as a policy holder are not professionals. Never hire someone until you've gathered your wits and taken charge of the situation as much as possible."

RENTER'S INSURANCE

The owner of any property is responsible for insuring the building. If you rent an apartment or a house, you are responsible for insuring your personal property and for additional living expenses. Renter's insurance will cover these costs. "Get renter's insurance even if you rent from a family member. If there is a loss, the homeowner will be dividing up the insurance money among other household members. You might receive more if you have your own policy," cautions Moss, a renter in a home that burned in a California firestorm.

TREES AND INSURANCE

"We get more calls surrounding the confusion of tree-related claim damages than on any other single homeowner's insurance claim. Consumers need a better understanding of tree-related damages and the coverage available," reports Solomon Green, a senior insurance investigator with the state of Georgia. Did you know that you might be covered if a tree falls on your house, but if it falls in your yard, you can be out of luck? Your homeowner's insurance will cover only damage to insured property (i.e., the house).

"We survived the ice storm. But we did not survive the trees. A huge tree fell on the house, the driveway and the yard. It made a whole in the roof, took down the power lines, crumbled the driveway to bits, and put a crater in our front lawn. Insurance paid for removal of the tree from the house, but the rest of the costs came out of my pocket," reports Marcia Hopkins, whose neighborhood in North Carolina was hit by a major ice storm.

Only trees lost to fire, explosion, lightning, rain, ice, snow and other specifically named perils are covered by homeowner's insurance. In many states "wind" is not one of the perils allowed. It can cost thousands of dollars to cut up a fallen tree, have it removed from your yard, repair the ground, and plant a new tree. If you have trees that are old or unhealthy, they are particularly vulnerable during bad weather. Consider consulting with an arborist about whether to remove them.

EARTHQUAKE AND FLOOD INSURANCE

There is no such thing as "disaster insurance," per se, that will cover you for every natural disaster, but there is insurance for earthquakes and floods. Earthquake and flood insurance is expensive. You and your family must decide now, before disaster strikes, if carrying earthquake insurance is a good idea. Deena McClain is well acquainted with the dilemma. She lives in a section of California known for earthquakes, floods, mudslides and wildfires. "Paying lots of money every year for disaster insurance is depressing, but losing everything with no insurance is even worse," she laments, so her family has earthquake insurance. Since the beginning of the Twentieth Century, earthquakes have occurred in 39 states. The Earthquake Education Center at Charleston Southern University claims that there is a 40%-60% chance of a major earthquake in the United States within the next 20 years—and approximately 90% of Americans live in seismically active areas.

Earthquake insurance is optional; however, if you live in an area that is at high risk for floods, flood insurance may be required when you buy a home. If you live in an area at high risk for floods and you don't have flood insurance, your homeowner's insurance will not protect you. Federally declared flood zones are rapidly expanding to cover new areas in New York, Florida, North Carolina and other states. Check with www.fema.org to determine if you are required to purchase flood insurance.

Two strategies to keep the cost of the premiums down are:

- Increase your deductible
- Implement mitigation steps (see Chapter Six). Your insurance company may lower your premium even for small mitigation efforts like securing your water heater to the wall.

AUTOMOBILE INSURANCE

Comprehensive coverage is that portion of your automobile insurance that pays for damage to your vehicle resulting from fire, vandalism, water, hail, glass breakage, wind, falling objects, civic commotion or hitting a bird or an animal. There are many restrictions and special circumstances applied to the terms *fire*, *water*, and *wind*, however, so be sure to check with your insurance carrier before assuming you are covered.

TERRORISM INSURANCE

The Terrorism Risk Insurance Act of 2002 ("The Act") was signed into law by President George W. Bush on November 26, 2002. The Act provides a federal backstop for certain acts of terrorism via a temporary federal program that distributes the risk of loss from foreign terrorist attacks between the federal government and the insurance industry. This federal backstop program is designed to ". . . protect consumers by addressing market disruptions and ensure the continued widespread availability and affordability of property and casualty insurance for terrorism risk." The Act covers only those terrorism events that are certified by the Secretary of the Treasury, in concurrence with the Secretary of State and the Attorney General of the United States. In order to qualify for certification, a terrorism event must meet the following criteria:

- The act must be a violent act dangerous to human life, property or infrastructure.
- The act must have resulted in damage within the United States (with some exceptions).

- The act must have been committed by an individual or individuals acting on behalf of a foreign person or foreign interest as part of an effort to coerce the civilian population of the United States or to influence the policy or affect the conduct of the United States Government by coercion.

The Act applies only to commercial property and casualty insurance policies, including worker's compensation policies. The Act also does not apply to personal insurance policies, such as homeowners' policies, private mortgage insurance, title insurance and personal automobile policies, neither does The Act apply to any health insurance policies or life insurance policies.

LIFE INSURANCE

Review your life insurance policy to be certain that those you leave behind are adequately provided for, whether your death is due to a disaster or not.

What Kids Can Do

- Insurance is "grown-up" business. But you can teach your kids what it means to take care of and protect their belongings. Teach them how putting their toys away will keep them from breaking. Buy keepsake boxes, display cases or other special containers that help them choose and protect what is most valuable to them.

CHAPTER FIVE

Protect the Contents of Your Home

If I Only Knew Then What I Know Now... *"I've been in the disaster preparedness field for over 20 years. With the exception of entrapment or death, the most heartbreaking scenes I've seen are people picking through soot, charred wood, and garbage to recover an old photograph or an ancestor's ring. A human life is nothing in comparison to these 'things.' It's heartbreaking, all the same, to see people searching for family keepsakes. They think 'It can never happen to me,' but believe me, disaster strikes randomly and it can happen to you. Take the steps you need to preserve your most cherished memories."* — Lynne Keating, professional risk communicator

DECLUTTER YOUR HOME

The less stuff in your home, the less you have to protect, inventory, insure, and replace. More importantly, clutter-free hallways, exits, and doorways can mean the difference between life and death if you have to escape from your home.

See Chapter Six for more information about decluttering.

A professional organizer can help you declutter your home and organize your possessions in a practical and attractive manner. You can reach a professional organizer by contacting the National Association of Professional Organizers at www.napo.net.

PROTECT YOUR COMPUTER AND ELECTRONIC INFORMATION

Your computer can take an indirect hit the moment electrical power goes out (which is common during many disasters), especially if you're writing data to the hard drive. Your information can get scrambled, and you'll probably lose what you've been working on. Worse, your hard drive may get fried. Power comes back on with a voltage surge that can harm your PC's circuits, sometimes even frying your main circuit board.

Make sure that you have a surge suppressor, and not just a power strip. A surge suppressor senses sudden surges in voltage and "clamps down" on it to keep it from reaching your computer, in effect, shutting down your system. Buy one with a power rating of at least 450 joules or higher, a minimum clamping voltage of 400 volts, and a response time of 10 nanoseconds or less. A joule is to a surge suppressor what wattage is to lightbulbs; it is a measure of power. Make sure it is UL-certified. Surge suppressors may burn as they take the current that would otherwise go to your computer, but they rarely catch fire. Replace your surge suppressor if it has burned.

A UPS might be a better way to protect your data. It contains a rechargeable battery that plugs into a wall outlet; the computer then plugs into an outlet on the UPS strip. When the power dies, the UPS automatically kicks in and supplies enough power to your PC to keep it going for up to two hours—if you've bought a top quality product. This will enable you to complete and save the projects you've been working on. You can also use a UPS on answering machines, cell phone chargers, copy machines, fax machines or any other equipment powered by electricity. For more information about UPS see Chapter Six.

If you're aware that there's a power outage, unplug the power cord even if you have a surge protector, and wait 20 minutes before turning the computer back on to avoid another surge. Always turn your computer off overnight and before going on vacation in the event of a nighttime storm or a spike in electricity that might occur in your absence.

> **TIP** Back up your data regularly so you don't lose it due to disasters or any other reason.

CONDUCT A HOME INVENTORY

When disaster strikes, it's simply not possible to take the contents of your home with you to safer quarters. A disastrous situation may cause you to lose your home and everything in it, or the contents of your home may be damaged or destroyed even if the home is repairable. A home inventory makes it possible for you to place a claim with your homeowners insurance for the replacement value of your possessions. It enables you to prove what you owned and its value. A well documented household inventory often results in claims being settled more quickly. You'll need documentation of your losses if you plan to write them off on your federal income tax returns. A home inventory has the added benefit of causing you to think about irreplaceable possessions that you may want to protect now. You might have uninsured artwork or rare and one-of-a-kind photographs for which no negative exists. You may want to consider scanning these to a disc (see Protecting Photographs below). The inventory also has the added advantage of getting you to think about your estate and what you'd like to leave selectively to your heirs.

A home inventory actually has two parts: the video recording or photography series, and a written inventory that documents the make, model, serial numbers, and estimated value of your possessions.

THE WRITTEN INVENTORY

A written inventory is the companion to your video recording. Do the written inventory first using the Home Inventory form in the Appendix then do the recording. If you have a large collection of videos, DVDs, books, record albums or other media, you may want to consider purchasing a special software program designed to inventory and index your collections. You can also use a home inventory software program rather than the manual forms provided in the Appendix, but remember to print out a hard-copy version.

If your only copy is on your computer it is vulnerable to data loss or damage especially during a disaster.

Attach receipts to the inventory for expensive items. If you don't have the receipt, attach advertisements for the exact item or a comparable ad. Remember to enter new major purchases as you make them onto the written inventory and keep the receipts.

THE RECORDING

If you're a good photographer and can capture detail, and if your written inventory is comprehensive, doing a photographic series of your home inventory is one option. Photographs and negatives, if properly stored, are actually more stable than video recordings or digital video cassettes. Also, the negatives prove that the original photograph has not been tampered with. Insurance companies and the courts are increasingly suspicious of digital images because they know they can be computer-manipulated. For added protection, transfer the photographs to a compact disc (CD) and note the date of the inventory on the CD.

Two other options are video recording or a digital video camera. The advantage of these media is that the visual recording of your home inventory is accompanied by audio. The audio can record descriptions of each item. If you do a video or digital recording, use the date feature on your camera to substantiate the date you established the value of the recorded items.

As you record each possession, read into the audio the following:

- Name of the item
- Brief description
- Brand name or manufacturer
- Serial or model number
- Where it was purchased or obtained
- Date of purchase or age
- The current value or replacement cost

Record one room at a time. Start at the entrance and record in a circular motion back to the entrance. Be sure to include the walls, ceilings, and floor so that you record artwork, chandeliers, carpeting, draperies and other items that are easy to overlook. Remember to do the following:

- Record the contents of your garage, closets, storage areas and home office.
- Include furniture, electronic equipment, major appliances, luggage, carpet, drapes, flooring, lighting and decorative items. Even include your laptop and camera cases!
- Record inside small places like drawers and china cabinets.
- For clothing, estimate the number of items you own by age and by category, for instance, 6 adult coats, 10 pairs of children's shoes, 12 teen shirts, 20 infant outfits, etc.) If you own expensive, designer clothing, record the designer's name and value of the clothing.
- Record lawn and patio furniture, landscaping, fencing, storage buildings (inside and out) and the pool.
- Record new major purchases as you make them.

HIRING SOMEONE ELSE TO DO YOUR HOME INVENTORY

If you don't own video or camera equipment or feel you don't have the skills or time, hire a home inventory service or a commercial video recording company with experience doing home inventories. Even if you do have the skills to do a home inventory, you may want to consider a more objective person doing it than yourself.

If you decide to go with a commercial company, check out their references. You don't want to take the chance that anyone will use the video maliciously. "Be sure they are bonded, licensed to do business in your community, and a member of the Better Business Bureau," Rick Bell of KC Home Inventory, Inc. recommends. A recent news story reported a fraudulent company that made video inventories and used them to arrange for home break-ins.

The biggest hurdle was listing my possessions from memory. I filled in about fifty pages of forms, with ten to twelve items on each page. My losses totaled between $600,000 and $700,000. I estimate insurance will cover $550,000 . . . in a way it feels good to be free and clear . . . I'm renting a place, and may not buy another house after all . . . The world is full of possibilities.—Barry Mohr who lost everything in the 2003 California wildfires

> aking an inventory may not sound like a difficult task but it can soon seem daunting because many of your possessions have memories and emotions associated with them that may slow up the process.—*Rick Bell*

Keep the recorded and written inventory in your safe deposit box. If you don't have a safe deposit box, keep it in your grab & go bag. Make a duplicate copy and mail it to a trusted friend for safekeeping. A good inventory service will offer to keep a backup copy at their premises. Be wary of online inventory services that promise you can simply download your inventory from their website. These web services tend to go in and out of business without much warning, taking your inventory with them!

PROTECTING MEMORABILIA

Memorabilia are items you cherish that may not have any monetary value, but are irreplaceable. Examples of memorabilia include wedding mementos, love letters, prized drawings from your kids, family Bibles and heritage photographs.

Treat your memorabilia as valuables. Store them in archival quality containers, boxes, albums or envelopes to prevent fading and deterioration, and to protect them from other hazards.

Elaine Sexton, a professional organizer in Florida, gives special emphasis to protecting memorabilia when she organizes her client's home. She says, "I make it a point to tell people to store their memorabilia so they can grab it in an emergency situation. My recommendation is to use empty suitcases to store your memorabilia. Choose the kind of suitcases with casters on them and stow them under your bed. During a hurricane, I grabbed suitcases from under the bed and wheeled them right into the car. I felt good knowing my cherished memories were safe with me."

PROTECTING PHOTOGRAPHS

Heritage Photographs

Heritage photographs are those that document your family's ancestry and exist only as an original photograph. Margaret Head's worst memory of Hurricane Andrew was her destroyed home. Her second worst memory was about her family photographs. "My one regret was not taking pictures off the walls. Those old family pictures were irreplaceable and one-of-a-kind and were all ruined by water damage. On a positive note, knowing how very important my pictures were to me, I kept negatives in a fire-protected box and had wrapped my photo albums in trash bags. So at least those were all safe and dry. I was thrilled that I didn't lose these treasured possessions," Margaret comments.

Storage of Photographs

Jena Blackshear, a professional photographer, recommends that you scan your heritage photographs onto a compact disc (CD) to preserve the image in digital form. When you print out the image from the CD, it prints exactly like the original or even better by using editing software that can diminish or remove stains, mend tears or folds, and repair other damage. Frame and display a copy from the CD and properly store the original.

In addition to preservation, CDs allow you to share your photos in a more convenient format than albums or actual photos. You can download the images to a disc and give the disc to anyone you like, or you can simply send the images themselves to someone else's computer. If you wish to preserve images from slides or negatives to a disc, you'll need a special scanner. CDs can last 100 years if stored in a cool, dry place, away from sunlight, and protected from scratches and mishandling. They won't survive a fire, tornado, or flood, however. For extra protection, store a copy of the CD in a safe deposit box or with an out-of-state relative.

Generations from now, will your descendants be able to access your CD? The technology for image storage is already changing and there are newer technologies to come, but the prognosis remains good that the images on a CD will be transferable to newer technologies such as digital video discs (DVD). The shelf life of a DVD is about the same as a CD, but a DVD has seven times the capacity of a CD. A single DVD can hold more than 15,000 photo-quality pictures, and transferring the images to a DVD is much faster than to a CD.

Once you transfer heritage photographs to CD or other media, store the originals in archival albums made of non-polyvinyl plastic with acid-free paper. Archival quality photo albums are chemically inert, which means photos won't dissolve, fade or deteriorate. Keep the albums (and individual photographs) away from heat sources such as lamps and sunlight and from humidity sources like water pipes. Of course, keep your photographs away from rodents, bugs and mold by making certain that your closets, drawers and all other storage areas for your photographs are clean and dry.

Some storage methods will actually contribute to the deterioration of your photographs because of the interaction between acid, lignin, and other harmful chemicals.

Never store heritage photographs in the following places:

- Shoeboxes
- Magnetic albums
- Manila or colored folders
- Plastic bags
- Film-developing envelopes

For photographs you'd like to display, consider hanging them high on a wall to avoid water damage. The glass in the frame should not touch the photograph, as glass and paper interact chemically in destructive ways. Use an acid-free mat, a non-wood frame (again to minimize chemical reactions), and leave the backing unsealed for ventilation. If you're lucky enough to have the negatives, store them in stainless steel or aluminum containers to prevent degeneration. The same applies to photographic slides.

The more centralized your photographs are, the easier they'll be to grab in an emergency. Store them separately from your negatives so that if you lose one, you might still have the other. If you have to evacuate immediately, leave the photographs behind. As hard as it may be, your family is most important, and seconds count if you must seek safety. Family and friends may have copies that they can duplicate for you. Eleven-year-old Melissa Harrison says, "My next door neighbor, Emily, is my best friend. We grew up together. Her home burned down during the wildfires. I'm glad she didn't go back in the house to get her pictures because she might have gotten hurt in the fire. Mom and I made an album of pictures of

Emily and her brothers and her parents from the pictures we had. Emily and her mom cried when we gave it to them."

Depending on the damage, you may be able to restore your photographs with the help of a conservator. Salvage the photographs; clean soiled pictures with a soft brush to remove soil, glass fragments, or other substances that can scratch or mar the surface. Do not use water or solvents. Carefully place each piece in a polyester sleeve or archival quality sleeve. Do not use any adhesive tape. If your photographs are water damaged, drain them off and put each one in a zipper-style plastic bag in the freezer, as freezing delays mold and mildew. If you cannot freeze them, place the photos between layers of paper towels and weigh them down under a heavy, flat object.

TIP Consider storing the actual heirloom photographs in an archival container and displaying only high-quality copies.

What Kids Can Do

- Choose prized drawings or mementos for special protection
- Help to photograph or video household items
- Declutter their rooms including donating old toys and clothes

CHAPTER SIX

Mitigation

Preparing Your House to Withstand Disaster

If I Only Knew Then What I Know Now... *"The weather radio said we had about fifteen minutes before the hurricane winds would hit our area. My family was already down in the basement. I ran outside and tied down the boat. As I headed for the basement stairs, a lawn chair came crashing through the window and knocked me on the head! Luckily, I was not too badly injured. We stayed in the safety of the basement till we got the 'all clear' to come out. And when we came out, the boat was okay, the lawn furniture had crashed through the windows, the kayak was up in a tree, and the doghouse was three houses away with the dog still in it! Next time, everything that can fly away gets loaded into the boat before it's roped down, except the dog!"* — Mark Holloway, Hurricane Isabel, Florida

Obviously, Mark could not prevent Hurricane Isabel, but you can prevent your property from adding to the destruction and injury that disasters can cause. These precautions are known as mitigation steps. Mitigation steps assure that your property:

- Does not add to destruction and injury
- "Weathers the storm" with as little damage as possible
- Recovers as quickly as possible

Some mitigation steps are non-structural such as installing basic fire equipment. Other mitigation steps require minor structural changes like making sure roof shingles are tight. Major structural changes such as replacing shingles with fireproof roofing materials can be implemented when you are building or moving into a new home or renovating your existing home. As an added bonus to the safety your family will enjoy, even the simplest of mitigation steps, such as installing smoke detectors, can lower your homeowner's insurance premium. Bigger improvements, like fire-resistant roofs, can lower premiums even more. Check with your insurance carrier. Make certain your home is up to building codes. If your home is below code, it may suffer even more damage during a disaster.

MITIGATING AGAINST FIRE DAMAGE

You may think of your house as a home, as a shelter, or as your castle, but a fire "thinks" of your house as fuel. Once it engulfs your home, a fire may gain the strength and energy it needs to spread to everyone else's home. The single most important mitigation step you can take is to install basic fire equipment in your home. Basic fire equipment is as essential to your home as toilets and includes smoke detectors, heat detectors, fire extinguishers, and escape ladders. The presence of properly working smoke and heat detectors, for instance, doubles your chance of survival in the event of fire.

SMOKE AND HEAT DETECTORS

What's the difference between smoke detectors and heat detectors? According to Sheri Lynch, a fire prevention educator, "A smoke detector detects the products of a fire, including smoke and rising dust. A heat detector detects heat. Generally speaking, smoke reaches the detectors more quickly than the heat. In a house fire at night, when people are sleeping, a smoke detector will give extra time to get out. That's why smoke detectors should be placed outside of sleeping areas," she explains. "However, in some locations, a *heat* detector is more appropriate. For example, it is not a good idea to put a smoke detector in the kitchen, as anyone who burns toast knows! A heat detector works best in a kitchen, because airborne grease particles and smoke will not set it off. Also, in dusty areas such as a garage (where car exhaust is also present) or an attic, heat detectors are a better choice than smoke detectors."

Smoke detectors should be installed:
- on each level of your home (at least one on each level),
- over the doorways outside each sleeping area,
- in the attic, and
- at the head of the basement stairs.

Heat detectors should be installed:
- in the basement near the furnace or water heater,
- in the kitchen,
- in the garage, and
- in other areas where dust, grease, smoke or fumes might set off a smoke detector.

Battery-operated smoke detectors require more frequent inspection than electrical smoke detectors that are wired directly into the power source of your home, but when the electricity goes out, battery-operated smoke detectors will continue to operate. Electrical smoke detectors will continue to operate only if they have a battery backup. Both kinds have a hush-button feature that silences a false alarm once the air clears, and they both automatically reset the alarm. Both have a light that indicates whether the alarm is functioning or not, and both have a test button.

HOW TO TEST YOUR SMOKE DETECTOR

Once a month, brush or vacuum the unit to keep it free of dirt, dust and cobwebs, which sometimes cause false alarms. Afterwards, use a broom handle and push the test button. You are testing to see if the battery is strong enough to set off the alarm. To test if the unit itself is efficient at detecting smoke after you are sure that the battery is working, light three wooden matches. Blow out the flame and let the smoke rise toward the unit. The smoke should set it off. Clear the air by waving away the smoke or by misting the smoke detector with water. Twice a year, replace the batteries. Be proactive—don't wait for the batteries to chirp. We tend to ignore such low level annoyances. If the batteries test well, use them somewhere else, but replace the batteries in the detectors twice a year anyway. Replace the unit itself every 10 years.

> **TIP** Tie the battery replacement to daylight saving time. Whenever you turn your clocks back or forward, change your smoke detector batteries.

If your smoke detector doubles as the toast-is-burning alarm, but there is no fire, mist the air beneath the smoke detector with a watering bottle. It will turn the alarm off. Don't remove the batteries to disengage the alarm, because it's too easy to forget to replace them again. Consider replacing the smoke detector with a heat detector.

FIRE EXTINGUISHERS

Fire extinguishers come in various classes. For your family's protection, a multi-class extinguisher labeled A-B-C is best. Install a fire extinguisher every 600 square feet of living space plus one in the kitchen, garage, basement, work-

How to Operate a Fire Extinguisher

The best way to remember the proper use of the fire extinguisher is to memorize the word **PASS**, which means:

Pull the pin.
Aim at base of fire.
Squeeze handle or trigger.
Sweep base of fire side to side starting with the end of the fire closest to you.

Be sure the pressure gauge is high, the lock pin is in place, and the nozzle is not clogged. When using a fire extinguisher, have an exit behind you so that you can get out of the house quickly. Never test a fire extinguisher by actually pulling the pin or squeezing the trigger. This lowers the pressure. Once per month check the pressure gauge. If it's low, recharge it. If it is the type that cannot be recharged, replace it. Follow the instructions on the fire extinguisher for proper disposal of spent fire extinguishers.

room or utility room, and in the bedroom of any smoker. Never use a Class A fire extinguisher on a grease fire. Class A fire extinguishers contain water, which will only cause the grease and fire to splatter and spread!

Classes of Fire Extinguishers:

- Class A will extinguish wood, paper, and standard combustible fires
- Class B is suitable for flammable liquids such as grease, gasoline, and oil
- Class C is designed for electrical fires
- Class K is for commercial cooking appliances that use fats and oils

ESCAPE LADDERS

Fire takes the same common path that people take—the stairs. Many homes have only a single staircase, so taking the stairs can be deadly. Emergency escape ladders offer a safer option. There are basically two kinds of fire escape ladders. One kind fits snugly over the windowsill and is stored rolled up, ready to be unrolled and pitched out the window. The other kind is

affixed to the wall stud itself and is stored in a small cabinet resembling a medicine cabinet under the window.

Photograph courtesy of Bold Industries, Inc.

Both are designed to support 600 to 1000 pounds of weight, the equivalent of three or four people going down the ladder at once. You'll have to decide which kind is right for your family. If your children are young or your household includes elderly or disabled family members, the cabinet version may be too difficult to operate.

Be aware of the following when purchasing an escape ladder:

- Choose a length according to the window height where you plan to exit. Remember that the longer the ladder, the more it weighs, and the more it weighs, the more difficult it is to pitch out the window.
- Make certain the steps are grooved for better traction.
- The wider the step width, the better (12 inches is good).
- Pay attention to the space between steps. If it is too deep, it may be too difficult for small children or elderly people.
- Assure that the last rung is a bright yellow or orange to indicate that you are near the ground.
- Be sure the instruction card is affixed to the ladder itself.

Practice a fire drill at home at least annually, more if the season is stormy, or if your area is susceptible to seasonal wildfires.

CREATE A SAFETY ZONE

Every house should have a defensible area around it with room for a fire truck. Fire personnel and equipment need to be able to move around your home with access to porches and decks. This area is called a safety zone, an area created around your home that separates it from combustible plants and vegetation. Walk the area around your house as if you were a firefighter, or better yet, walk around your home *with* a firefighter! Many fire departments allow personnel to do fire safety inspections of homes in their area. Call the administrative office of your local fire department to find out if this service is available. If your local fire department has this service for free, be certain to make a donation to the Fireman's Fund in exchange. If this service is not offered, many firefighters provide this service, for a fee, on their days off from work.

Follow these tips to create a safety zone:

- Clear brush, shrubbery, plants, trees and bushes away from your house.
- Remove dead limbs, pine needles, dying moss and dead trees from your property.
- Prune branches so they are not in contact with the house. Fire can run across tree branches like a squirrel on a telephone wire.
- Make certain fire equipment can easily pull up to your home.
- Use tile, stucco, slate or other fire-resistant material for your roof instead of wooden shakes and shingles, if at all possible.
- Clean your gutters regularly to prevent trapped material from burning and also to keep rainwater away from your house. Rainwater can be very corrosive and weaken the entire structure of a house.
- Replace doors between your house and your garage or carport with doors that have a fire rating of one-hour or greater.
- Inside the house, remember that fabric and heat do not mix. Keep furniture away from fireplaces and space heaters, keep drapes away from baseboard heaters and keep towels away from bathroom heat lamps.

TIP Be sure your house number is clearly visible at night so that fire and other emergency vehicles can find your home.

MITIGATING AGAINST TREES AND WIND DAMAGE

William R. McNutt, Sr., whose career in disaster preparedness spanned more than thirty years has seen it all. "It's amazing how much damage the wind can cause to a home. I've seen swing sets blown through the living room wall, patio furniture tossed through the window of the den, and swimming pool equipment in the second floor bedroom. Once I saw a cow blown onto the top of a river bridge trestle! If the wind can blow a cow fifty feet up in the air, imagine what it can do with your kid's playhouse," cautions McNutt. Large trees with thick foliage can act as sails in high winds, capturing the wind. If the wind can't blow through the branches, it will simply push over a tree with a weak foundation. Thin out your trees by removing some of the branches throughout. You may need an arborist to assist you, but it's well worth the expense. A large tree can crush a house, shatter a driveway, or destroy a yard or pool. It can fall as a result of wind, fire, drought, or many other reasons.

PROTECTION FROM LIGHTNING

Lightning can cause fires, explosions or electrical surges. If you live in an area prone to frequent or severe thunderstorms, installing a lightning protection system, which is designed to protect a building from fires caused by lightning. Lightning protection systems consist of lightning rods called "points," down conductors that are large stranded wires, and two or more ground rods, and provide protection by conducting a lightning charge safely into the ground. These systems do not protect electronic systems or electronic equipment—for that you'll need a surge protector. Your lightning protection systems should meet UL and National Fire Protection Association (NFPA) standards. The installation company should also be UL certified.

Surge protection devices are designed to protect sensitive electronic equipment and devices. In fact, the owner's manuals of most electronic devices recommend surge protection, and, in some cases, it is required by warranties. Connect any sensitive electronic devices to a surge protector, including computers, TVs, washers, dryers, ovens, microwaves, garage door openers and audio equipment. Don't forget to protect the phone line(s) and cable TV connections by purchasing a plug-in surge protector with phone and cable TV surge protection. "When purchasing plug-in surge protectors, be sure the surge protector has a UL1449 330V listing. If it doesn't, don't buy it," advises John West, President of Power & Systems Innovations in Florida, a state beset with many electrical storms.

In addition to lightning protection systems and surge protectors, if your area is prone to electrical storms, consider installing ground fault circuit interrupters (GFCI) to protect from shocks. GFCIs trip when there is any indication that electrical current is going where is it not supposed to go. Chances are they have already been installed near electrical receptacles within four feet of sinks, exterior plugs, and near tubs and showers if you live in an area prone to electrical storms. Check with your power company to be sure.

Use a UPS to operate electrical equipment and appliances by battery if your electrical power is out. A confusing array of these products is on the market. West recommends you find out the following information before purchasing and installing a UPS:

- What is the voltage of the connected equipment?
- What is the total amperage draw of the equipment?
- What is the minimum runtime needed on battery?
- Does the equipment include any "motor" loads, such as electric motors or pumps?

Consult the website of UPS manufacturers. Many provide runtime charts on their websites and tools to calculate the size UPS you need.

MITIGATION AGAINST ELECTROCUTION HAZARD

Water can weaken the structure of your home. It can seep into the lowest floors where many homes have their electrical systems. Chances are you won't drown in your home, but you may be at risk for electrocution. Many people survive a disastrous water event only to be electrocuted by electrically charged wet surfaces. Mitigate the danger from electricity and water by taking these steps.

- Raise circuit breakers, fuse boxes, utility meters, furnaces and water heaters to higher elevations to avoid wetness.
- Consider relocating electric, telephone and cable lines to the upper level of your home.
- In new home construction, considering putting heating, ventilating and air conditioning units in the upper story or attic.
- Avoid downed power lines.
- Seal basement walls with waterproofing compounds.

EARTHQUAKE MITIGATION

There is a 40-60% chance of a major earthquake in the United States within the next 20 years, according to The Earthquake Education Center, and about 90% of Americans live in seismically active areas. Mitigate the damage from earthquakes by taking the following steps:

- Make sure your roof is firmly secured to the main frame of the house.
- Be sure roof shingles are secured to the roof itself.
- Attach the gas water heater to the wall with metal strapping or nylon to keep it from shifting. If the gas water heater is stable, the gas line will not break and cause a fire hazard.
- Cover pipes during cold spells so they don't burst.
- Move to low shelves any heavy or breakable objects.

TIP Check with your local office of Federal Emergency Management to see if your home qualifies for special mitigation loans or grants.

FLOOD MITIGATION

The most effective flood mitigation step is to determine if you live on a flood plain. Contact your local emergency management office or check your state's emergency management website. If you live on a flood plain, consider living at higher elevations and be sure to purchase adequate flood insurance (see Chapter Four).

STORE GASOLINE PROPERLY

Gasoline is a highly volatile liquid giving off vapors that can easily be ignited by a spark, flame or hot object. The vapor of one cup of gasoline has the explosive power of about five pounds of dynamite. Store gasoline in containers with a UL or Factory Mutual (FM) rating. UL and FM are non-profit, product safety testing and certification organizations that are independent of the product manufacturers. If you must transport gasoline, use a UL-approved container and secure it so it does not slide around or tip over. Once you get it home, store the container in a well ventilated area separate from the house where there are no sources of spark, flame or heat.

CONTROL YOUR UTILITIES

"Utilities" refers to the sources of electrical power, natural gas and water in your home. Every house has a way to turn these on and off. In apartments, the building superintendent controls the utilities. Under certain disaster conditions, you'll need to be able to turn particular utilities off and back on again. Mitigate the effects of a disaster by knowing how to control your utilities during a disaster.

The Water Main Valve

Turn off the water main valve if the water pipes become damaged or if local authorities advise you to. When you turn off the water main valve, you are preventing water from draining away in case the water main itself breaks. Turning off the water will prevent a dangerous decrease in water pressure, flooding, water damage, and the potential for wet surfaces to come in contact with electricity. The water main valve is located in the lower portion of the house. Once you locate it, label the water main itself and identify the water main valve with a large tag. Be sure you lubricate the water valve once a year.

Electricity

There are two disaster-related circumstances under which you may need to voluntarily turn off the electricity to your home: if water is around your electric meter, and if advised to do so by disaster officials.

In most homes, electrical service comes into the house through power lines, passes through an electric meter and goes into the control panel, sometimes called a breaker box or fuse box. Usually the control panel is near the electric meter, close to where the power lines enter the house. The control panel controls the electricity that travels along all the electrical circuits in the house. If you have an older home, the control panel will have fuses. Individual fuses correspond to individual circuits such as the electric range. One or two handles in the control panel can turn off the electricity in the whole house. New homes have circuit breakers. The main breaker turns off the electricity in the whole house. Other circuit breakers may control the air conditioning system or other devices.

TIP Attach a flashlight near the control panel with Velcro®. Label the fuses and circuit breakers so that you know which electrical appliance or device it corresponds to.

Natural Gas

Natural gas is highly explosive and plays a frightening role in disasters. An earthquake can rupture a gas main, filling the entire neighborhood with highly combustible gas. Even small amounts of methane (the natural gas most homes utilize) can be ignited from tiny, static electricity sparks that can come from dialing a telephone or from a ringing a doorbell.

Usually, the gas main valve is located outside the house where the gas line from the street enters your house. Using a dual combination wrench designed for both gas and water shut-off, turn the gas off. A turn to the right, or clockwise, closes the gas off. A turn to the left, or counterclockwise, opens the gas line. Once you've located it, tag it with a label.

Courtesy of Utili-Tag

Utili-Tag™ is a product that includes all the labels any household might need for labeling utilities. It's available at www.util-itags.com. Another unique product, called the 4-in-1 Emergency tool™ can shut off the water main, shut off the gas, pry open doors, and dig through debris. It's available at www.onduty1.com.

What To Do If There Is a Gas Leak

Methane gas is odorless, but you can detect a gas leak through an odor that the gas company purposely puts in the gas. It smells like bad eggs or sulfur.

If the odor is faint, open the windows, and investigate the source. Check your gas stove first. If you cannot find the source and the odor is still faint, you can turn your gas off or contact the gas utility company to investigate the situation.

If the odor is strong, get out of the house. Open windows and doors on your way out. Do not use anything that might ignite a spark, such as using any kind of phone (including a cell phone), light switch or car ignition. Call the gas company from a neighbor's house or from your car. Stay outside until the gas company says its safe to return.

Once you have turned the gas off, only the gas company can safely turn the gas back.

CARBON MONOXIDE

Carbon monoxide (CO) is an invisible, odorless, poisonous gas produced by the incomplete combustion of fuels like gasoline, kerosene, propane, natural gas, oil or wood. Carbon monoxide is the number one cause of poisoning deaths in America. If you have a fuel-burning appliance of any kind, such as a fireplace, wood-burning stove or kerosene lamps, install a CO detector. Install one on each floor of the hour, near the bedrooms where the sound of the alarm will be heard. Prevent CO by professionally checking the chimney and furnace.

If the alarm sounds, you should:

- get everyone out of the house
- call 911
- get immediate attention for anyone with signs of carbon monoxide poisoning (dizziness and headaches are common)

DO A MITIGATION/ HOME HAZARD HUNT

You and your children, depending on their age, can conduct a home hazard and mitigation hunt to be sure you have done all you can to mitigate against injury and destruction during a disaster. Refer to Appendix for the Home Hazard Hunt and Mitigation Checklist.

DECLUTTER YOUR HOME

The contents of your home may be your fondest possessions, but in a disaster, ordinary items in and around your home can become deadly missiles, dangerous explosives and destructive obstructions that can injure not only you or your family, but also others around you. Household clutter can make it difficult to exit your home in an emergency. Clutter in the garage, attic or other storage areas is added fuel for fires, and clutter can cause household accidents any time of the year, not just during disasters.

- Remove clutter from stairways, doorways and windows.

- Eliminate excess "stuff" from your closets, garage, attic and other storage areas.
- Donate unused clothing, household goods and other items to charity.

A professional organizer can help you de-clutter and organize your home. You can reach a professional organizer by contacting the National Association of Professional Organizers at www.napo.net.

MITIGATION AND TERRORISM

Mitigating terrorism is a complex subject involving politics, conflict resolution, national security, and many issues. That said, the risk to you and your family and your individual home due to terrorism is very small because the preferred targets of terrorists are not homes in residential communities in the United States. Terrorists target non-residential symbols of power, and large-scale structures that, if damaged, are capable of disrupting major infrastructures. Examples of these targets include airports, military installations and embassies. Worldwide, terrorists most commonly use explosives. Other kinds of terrorism include chemical and biological attacks, and nuclear and radiological attacks.

If you live near a potential terrorism target, and you are concerned about the risk of terrorism to your family, it may make more sense for you to move to another locality than to institute mitigation steps. You could take steps to protect your home against an explosive bombing by building a subterranean bomb shelter, but it would only serve to protect you with adequate advance warning of an attack. These kinds of steps could seriously change your lifestyle and may not even be legally permitted in your neighborhood. Given the small risk, it may not be worth your while to do anything extra to your home in anticipation of terrorism that would be different from steps you would take to mitigate natural disasters.

The Rand Corporation published a 2003 quick guide titled *Individual Preparedness and Response to Chemical, Radiological, Nuclear and Biological Terrorist Attacks*. It suggests that you can create a barrier against biological agents by weatherizing your home and install good quality particulate filters on heating and ventilation systems to help remove contaminants from indoor air.

Other mitigation steps include knowing how to escape from your home and evacuating to safe shelter. For information on these strategies see Chapter Ten.

What Kids Can Do

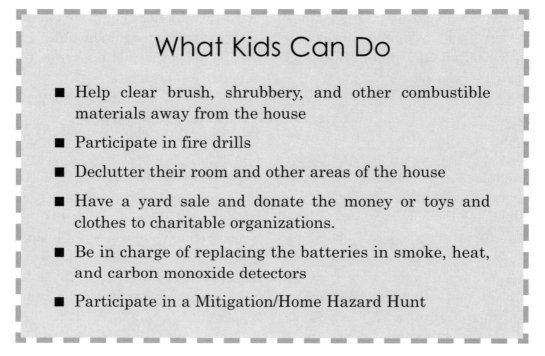

- Help clear brush, shrubbery, and other combustible materials away from the house

- Participate in fire drills

- Declutter their room and other areas of the house

- Have a yard sale and donate the money or toys and clothes to charitable organizations.

- Be in charge of replacing the batteries in smoke, heat, and carbon monoxide detectors

- Participate in a Mitigation/Home Hazard Hunt

CHAPTER SEVEN

Your Family Communication Plan

If I Only Knew Then What I Know Now...*A client of mine thought preparation was unimportant, that he would know what to do when the time came. Well, the time came, via a major hurricane, and his town was evacuated. He had no money with him; one of his children was out of state, but the other was in school near him; the battery to his cell phone was not charged. His ex-wife could not reach him and was in extreme panic that she did not know where her youngest child was or where their shelter was, which was different from her shelter. So many things could have been pre-planned but they weren't, so they were forced to live in anxiety for two days until they connected. With just one hour of pre-planning, they would have been able to connect immediately.* — Carol Schaer, Risk Manager

Reaching loved ones is one of the most anxiety-producing aspects of coping with a disaster. Not only do we worry about the safety of the people we love, but we are also eager to put them at ease about our own situation. Having a Family Communication Plan in place will help to alleviate the anxiety of contacting one another in an emergency.

During disasters, face-to-face communication of the kind your family is used to may be difficult or impossible. Your family may be working, going to school, shopping, etc., and they may be unable to reconvene at home in certain circumstances. Complicating the communication picture is the reality that telephone and e-mail may be unavailable. If your family has to rapidly escape from home, you'll need to be able to quickly account for everyone's safety outside the house. Use the form in the Appendix for your Family Communication Plan.

FAMILY REUNION SPOT

The first part of the plan is to decide in advance on a Family Reunion Spot, a place where your family will plan to meet if you are separated from each and disaster strikes your home. You want to make certain that everybody is accounted for, and that everyone has escaped from the house safely. This is important to put you at ease and to alert emergency personnel about missing family members. You certainly don't want emergency personnel rushing into your burning home to risk their lives if everyone is accounted for.

Choose a family reunion spot easy for everybody to walk to, but far enough away from the house as to not be dangerous. A neighbor's house up the street is a good choice, or a nearby school or mall. A place protected from the weather and well lit is advisable. Other choices include a neighborhood library, com-

munity center or place of worship. Record your family reunion spot on the Family Communication Plan using the form in the Appendix. If your entire neighborhood or other large areas are affected by disaster, you may need to meet out-of-town. This is covered in Chapter Ten.

ESTABLISHING PHONE CONTACT

The next part of the plan is to establish phone contact. During a power outage, the phone lines are often still working, because telephone companies supply their own electricity through the phone line and are not dependent on the same electrical grid or power plants as the lines that keep the lights on. *Depend on your landline phone as your primary command post during a disaster.* Cell phones work without electricity, but cell phones may not be working. Cell phone towers and antennas are fragile and may go down during certain disasters. Microwave links between cells and switching centers can go down, and, like land phones, cell phones can suffer from call volume overload that overwhelms the cell phone system.

Family members who are out of the house at the time of a disaster should attempt to call home. Someone from the family should be stationed at the phone, *if the house is safe*, as a kind of command post. Answer your land phone when it rings; don't let it roll over to your answering machine or other device. This will give you an opportunity to convey important information and to reassure the caller with the sound of your voice.

- Have working pens, as well as pencils and pads easily accessible near the phone.
- Affix a short list of emergency phone numbers to the bottom of or near your phone.
- Clear away the clutter from the area around your home phone.
- Program key phone numbers into the phone, including cell phone numbers, work phone numbers, your out of town contact, and phone numbers of family or friends to reach in any emergency.
- Know how to retrieve messages remotely and be sure everyone else knows how also.
- Write down critical information, such as where the family member is, when they called in last and at what number they can be reached.

If you are not home during a disaster, communication to your home may be severely limited or very unpredictable. If you reach your family, don't make a promise to call back in an hour, for example—that you may not be able to keep. It will only cause undue worry. Instead, promise to call back as soon as you can. Be brief and reassuring.

OUT-OF-TOWN CONTACT

During a disaster, your local telephone service may be non-operational, but frequently, long distance phone service is working. Local call lines can become overwhelmed by the quantity of phone calls being placed at the same time, but long distance calls have less "traffic." Establish a family contact that lives out-of-town. If your entire neighborhood is affected by a disaster and it is difficult to reconvene at your family reunion spot, you can reach your out-of-town contact and leave a message as to your whereabouts. Each family member can call into this contact and thereby establish a head count that you cannot accomplish in person.

Valuable information can be exchanged via your out-of-town

contact. Choose an out-of-town contact that is calm and can write messages down clearly. Enter this person's name and phone number on your Family Communication Plan and program their phone number into your phone. Make certain that the individual knows they have been chosen as your out-of-town contact.

OTHER IMPORTANT CONTACTS AND INFORMATION

Your place of employment might have a disaster plan of its own. It may be their policy to shelter-in-place and encourage employees not to journey home, depending on the circumstances. Check with your human resources office to understand your company's disaster plan and let your family know the policy. Determine the best way to keep yourself safe while optimizing contact with your family from work. Be certain your work phone number and the work numbers of every household member are on the Family Communication Plan.

Schools and day care centers generally have a disaster plan in place.

Learn what it is. You are most interested in knowing:

- under what circumstances your child will be held at the school or day care center and under what circumstances they will be released to go home;
- what kind of authorization the school or day care center requires to release your child to other adults if you cannot get there yourself;
- that the school or day care center knows your current contact information and the contact information of people authorized to collect your children for you; and
- that they have a copy of your Family Communication Plan.

Review and update the Family Communication Plan with your family at least once per year. An excellent time to do this is at the beginning of the new year or on a holiday weekend like Memorial Day or President's Day. The date doesn't matter as long as it's easy to remember and you do it annually. Mark it on your family calendar. An elevation of the HSAS threat level, or a severe weather forecast are other occasions to review and practice your plans. It's a good idea to review your Family Communication Plan in conjunction with practicing your evacuation plan. Store your written Family Communication Plan on the refrigerator or in another central family area in a transparent, red plastic document sleeve. A copy should be included in your grab & go bag.

COMMUNICATION TECHNOLOGY

Telephones

In the 1960s a TV program ran called *Get Smart* about a secret agent named Maxwell Smart. When his headquarters called him, he would take off his shoe and hold it up to his ear. In those days the idea of a shoe with a telephone in it was considered very high tech. Now phones can be found in wristwatches, wristwatches have e-mail, and radios and cameras are part of cell phones. Communication technology is changing all the time.

Dialing 911

Natural disasters and unnatural disasters do not affect one household; they affect a community or a geographic area. On the one hand, you want to be absolutely certain that 911 is contacted to protect the community. On the other hand, if everyone in the affected area calls 911 at the same time, the system

The development of a modern emergency response system, which later became known as 911, was the latest and greatest communication technology. The first emergency three-digit number was utilized in 1937 in Great Britain. In 1957, the National Association of Fire Chiefs in the United States recommended a nationwide, single emergency number, but it was not until 1967 that President Lyndon Johnson moved the initiative forward. He called upon the Federal Communications Commission (FCC) for a solution. The FCC met with American Telephone and Telegraph Company (AT&T), the phone monopoly. On January 12, 1968, AT&T announced the selection of 911 as the universal emergency number. It was selected for several reasons: it is brief and easy to remember, it can be dialed quickly, and it is not an existing area code or exchange.

can become overwhelmed. Use your judgment. If the disaster has just occurred and you are one of the first on the scene, calling 911 makes sense. If the disaster has been ongoing or is very widespread, chances are someone else has called. If you are at all in doubt or cannot decide whether or not to call 911, call.

911 and Children

Children as young as three-and-a-half can learn how to call 911. Teach them that 911 is used for emergencies only. An emergency is when you need help from a fire-fighter, a policeman, a doctor or an ambulance. Give them an example by role playing each kind of emergency scenario: a fire, an intruder and an unconscious family member (depending on their age this might mean a family member who "won't wake up").

- Teach them what is *not* an emergency: a skinned knee, a missing bicycle, a lost pet, and an argument with a sibling are examples.
- Always tell them to dial 9-1-1 not "nine eleven." Eleven is not a number on the phone dial and the child may become confused.
- If they are in doubt and there is no adult around, teach them not to hesitate to call.
- Teach them that the 911 operator is a friend and they can trust the operator.
- Teach children to convey your address *and* phone number. The phone number is especially important if they are on a cell phone. If the call gets dropped the 911 operator can call back.
- Teach them that if they call 911 as a prank or joke, it means someone else who is having an emergency may not be able to get help and the prank caller will be caught and punished.

Cell Phones

Half of all Americans now own cell phones and more and more of them rely on cell phones as their primary phone and own no land-line. Cell phones are very vulnerable during disasters. When local government attempts to convey disaster information by telephone, many people are not reachable.

When you talk on a cell phone, it picks up your voice and converts the sound to radio frequency or radio waves. The radio waves travel through the air until they reach a cell phone tower. The tower relays your call to a telephone network until it reaches the person you are calling. Much can happen to a cell phone call as it travels its route during a disaster. Rely on a landline phone as your command post phone.

Don't discount your cell phones altogether however, their mobility and convenience will come in very handy during an emergency, assuming they can pick up a signal. Talk time is the amount of time you can actually talk on your phone without recharging. Standby time is the amount of time your phone can be powered on without recharging the battery. The larger the actual size of the battery, the more talk time and standby time your phone will have without having to recharge the battery. Use the manufacturer's highest performance battery. "If consumers are concerned about having reliable cell phones in emergency situations, they need to pick a phone that is both digital and analog with lithium ion or lithium ion polymer batteries," notes Ray O'Rourke, a purchasing manager with the wireless division of a major phone distributor. Keep the batteries properly charged and have a spare.

TIP Newer models of cell phones let you use the keypad to enter a short text message. Although this takes up more battery power, a text message can get through even if an emergency overloads voice circuits.

Cell Phones and 911

When you get through, give your cell phone number immediately so that the operator can call you back if the call gets dropped. Give your location as exact as possible, including landmarks. "A lot of consumers assume that a 911 call from a cell phone is just as accurate as from a landline phone. It comes as a surprise to them that it is not," says Gregory Rohde, Executive Director of E911, a non-profit organization supporting enhancements to the 911 system. Equipping wireless networks to pinpoint the location of callers is a monumental task compared to landline phones that have fixed physical locations. Do not assume your locality has the most recent 911 optimization technology.

Here's what you can do to optimize your ability to reach 911 on a cell phone during a disaster:

- Purchase dual-band, tri-mode or multi-network cell phones that maximize the chances of reaching 911.
- When driving, keep your phone on and the antenna extended for the greatest "visibility" by cell towers.
- If you can't reach 911, try again. Another tower may pick up your call
- Use a digital and analog cell phone with the manufacturer's best lithium ion or lithium ion polymer batteries.

The Federal Communications Commission (FCC) regulations require that cell phone users be able to dial 911, *regardless of whether your cell phone has a phone number or service,* however there are some exceptions. Your cell phone carrier must have an arrangement with the Public Safety Answering Point (PSAP) of the FCC before the PSAP will relay the call to 911. Not every carrier has this arrangement so you might want to check with your carrier beforehand to determine its 911 policy.

If you have a cell phone you are not using and it can be charged up, bring it to your carrier and find out if you can use it for 911 emergencies. Even a totally dead cell phone can often be recharged from a charger or a car battery.

For more information about cell phones and 911, see the National Emergency Number Association's website at www.nena.org.

Emergency Phones

Many retailers sell "emergency only" phones, designed to be used to contact 911 only. They work on batteries, so buy a big supply if you intend to use these phones. The calls to 911 are free and are one-touch. They are lightweight and perfect for travel or for the elderly or people who may have physical difficulty dialing 911. Be aware that if you have taught your young children to dial 911 and then you introduce them to a one-touch phone, it may be confusing to them and their ability to dial 911 in other circumstances may be undermined. Older children already acquainted with dialing 911 can certainly use one-touch dialing.

Cordless Phones

A cordless phone can be a definite plus during an emergency, but a cordless phone is charged from the cradle or base where it sits, drawing on your home's electrical system. If your electrical power goes down, so does the cordless phone whereas your landline phone, bypasses your home's electrical system—another reason to have a landline phone as well as a cordless phone.

Prepaid phone cards

A prepaid phone card allows you to purchase a set amount of calling minutes that you can use on any telephone. Expect to pay between 3 cents and 20 cents per call, depending on the card. Prepaid cards can be used to make calls from a pay phone without coins, but you'll pay more. If you need to reach out-of-town contacts, prepaid phone cards may be less expensive than paying for long-distance calling charges. Prepaid phone cards are available in convenience stores, post offices, and many retail establishments. You can buy any phone card; it does not have to be one issued from your long-distance service provider, nor does the card obligate you to switch to a different local or long-distance provider. To place a call, simply dial the 800 number on the back of the card, enter a PIN number (also on the back of the card), and dial the number.

Voice Mail

Many phone companies offer voice mail service at an extra cost. With voice mail, you can create an outgoing "emergency" message and receive messages even if you are on the phone. You can even receive messages if the power is out and can check messages remotely from most locations. For more information, check with your phone company.

Computer

The Internet is critically important for conveying information, but it has its limitations. California Senator Barbara Boxer was asked how the public could be helped during recent wildfires in her state. She replied, "Forty-eight hundred of my constituents lost their homes or businesses. Emergency agencies are quick to set up websites that made essential information available about evacuation, how to file insurance claims, and other information, but I insisted that *physical* emergency centers be set up immediately. Peoples' homes have been burned to the ground. Do you really think they can get to their computers?"

According to *Entrepreneur Magazine*, "One of the most striking trends has been how quickly wireless networking has become a standard feature of portable computers of every size. A year ago, one in four notebooks had some kind of wireless networking. Today, three out of four do." Personal digital assistants (PDAs) are also very popular.

Wireless technology is clearly the wave of the near-future, but most people still rely on computers that plug into an electrical source or use a battery-operated laptop computer. If your DSL and cable modems go down with the electricity and your telephone line is intact, you can still use a dial-up connection on a battery-powered computer. Find out from your DSL or cable provider if they provide an auxiliary dial-up account. You'll be tempted to play games and run DVD movies on your battery power, but conserve it for more important uses like sending e-mail and looking up crucial disaster information on the Internet. If you do not have a laptop computer, your desktop computer can perform without electricity when connected to UPS.

If you are away from your own computer, you can still access your e-mail by using the Internet from any other computer, using a URL your internet service provider (ISP)

can give to you. For example, America Online allows access to any e-mail account via its website at www.aol.com. Contact your ISP for more information.

Ham Radios

Ham radio operators, also called amateur radio operators, can play vital roles during disasters. "Most people don't realize that whenever there is an emergency the first people responding are amateur radio operators," notes Bob Hejl, a member of the Amateur Radio Emergency Services.

"Hams supply vital and accurate communication until the local infrastructure can be rehabilitated. Many ham radio operators have off-line power that can communicate should the local power grid be disabled." Bob learned just how valuable his services were when he volunteered to assist at the World Trade Center in New York City on September 11, 2001. "Not having communications with ground zero until I arrived, the Red Cross headquarters needed an update on conditions pertaining to their temporary shelters in terms of food, cots, and water. I had no idea my 12-hour shift would last three days," recounts Bob.

Ham is a shortened version of home amateur. The transmissions of ham radios are at different frequencies than regular radio transmissions; therefore, they can operate even when other radio transmissions cannot. As Bob Hejl notes above, they can also communicate off the main power grid. A ham radio has a transmitter and a receiver called a transceiver. Voice (or data or Morse code) is transmitted over particular radio frequencies to antennas and received by other ham radios. The receiver can decode the information that is sent. Morse code beeps can often get through radio frequency when voice cannot, so ham operators can transmit information about disasters via Morse code to other ham operators who can then relay the information to disaster officials. Ham radio technology, like all technologies, is becoming more sophisticated with the use of satellites, improved transceivers and computerization. For more information about becoming a ham radio operator check the website www.arrl.org.

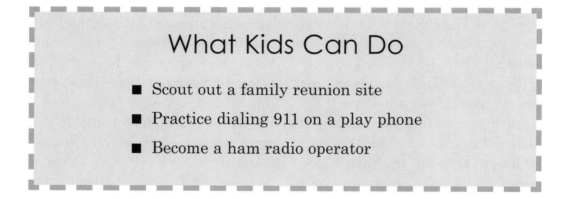

What Kids Can Do

- Scout out a family reunion site
- Practice dialing 911 on a play phone
- Become a ham radio operator

CHAPTER EIGHT

Family-Friendly First Aid

If I Only Knew Then What I Know Now... *"It was pretty frightening seeing all those people stumble out of the building with bleeding heads, gasping for air. I wished I could do more. There is no way to anticipate a thing like this . . who would have ever thought people would fly jets into the World Trade Center? Well, I stopped wishing about what I could do and I learned first aid. Now I feel confident that I can help my family or somebody else next time . . . if there ever is a next time."* — Jack Watson, 9/11 survivor, New York City

First aid is something you and your family can easily learn and it can save lives. When you rely on your own first aid knowledge to attend to common disaster-related injuries, you free up medical resources to attend to the more seriously injured. If emergency medical personnel don't have to make a stop at your house, that's another life-saving minute they can spend with people who cannot wait for medical assistance. Also, when your family knows first aid, they have confi-

dence in themselves. They will be less likely to panic in an emergency situation. An added benefit of first aid is that it will serve you well if you have to contend with injuries not associated with disasters, such as injuries caused by household or traffic accidents.

LEARNING FIRST AID

Preparedness is best served by having at least one person in your

Most of us are familiar with the term "first aid." But what does it really mean? Historically, first aid goes back to medieval England. The Order of St. John was formed in 1099 of religious knights trained in medical care to treat sick and wounded soldiers. The concept of civilian pre-medical treatment was introduced by Surgeon-Major Peter Shepherd, a member of the Order some seven hundred years later. Shepherd designed a special "litter" for carrying the wounded, which was named "The St. John Ambulance" and he established the Ambulance Corp. In those days, "ambulance" meant anything that could carry a person. The term "first aider" was coined in September 1894 by Dr. Heaton Howard, editor of the Order's journal *First Aid*. Even today, first aid still means care administered prior to medical treatment. The level of care that first aid delivers stabilizes the injured, preventing further damage and promoting recovery. It also enables assistance to be delivered to those in most medical need first.

family take a first aid course by a certified instructor. Basic first aid courses will teach you to respond to shock, cardiac, and breathing emergencies, heat and cold emergencies, sudden illnesses, and poisoning. You'll also learn to how to administer first aid to stop bleeding and treat broken bones, as well as treat cuts and scraps. Choose a course that is certified by the American Red Cross. That way you will receive instruction from experienced instructors with the latest skills. First aid courses are offered by certified instructors at many local hospitals, police departments, public health agencies and fire departments.

First aid basics can also be learned through self-study. Purchase a good quality first aid kit. Familiarize yourself with its contents, and study the first aid manual that is enclosed with it. Videos, CDs, and online courses are also first aid self-study methods. The main drawback of first aid self-study is that it is difficult for you to verify how well you are performing first aid methods and techniques without a trained instructor's supervision. Another drawback is that, although you will have the components of your first aid kit to practice with, you won't have the manikins and other props to practice on, which first aid courses provide.

Most first aid courses are combined with cardio-pulmonary resuscitation (CPR) instruction. They are about 10 hours long spread over a couple of days, and cost about $65. Review classes are about five hours long and in the range of $40. Be certain to take review classes periodically. Like any new skill, first aid knowledge is lost if not practiced or reviewed regularly.

COMMON DISASTER-RELATED INJURIES

The most common disaster is floods. Injuries related to floods include drowning, electrocution, hypothermia and illness from water contaminated with bacteria. Wind events like hurricanes and tornadoes cause bruises, lacerations, and broken bones from flying debris or falling structures and the added risk of bleeding from broken glass. Fires often result in burns and smoke inhalation, injuries that can be fatal. Other disaster-related health problems are caused by stress. For some people, anxiety attacks and heart attacks are the body's response to physical and emotional stress. Shock is a common, disaster-related health

problem. Most of us have felt our heart beat fast or become nauseous in an emergency, but full-fledged shock is a dangerous condition that can be fatal. It is unlikely that first aid instruction will cover each and every disaster-related injury in depth. But the skills gained from first aid instruction and the confidence you will have it knowing you can help, will make you of valuable assistance on any disaster scene.

FIRST AID AND TERRORISM

Most acts of terrorism involve bombings and explosives. Very few acts of terrorism worldwide have involved the use of chemical or biological agents or nuclear attack. Acquiring and deploying these methods is much more difficult than setting off explosives. According to Dr. Arthur Kellerman of the Department of Emergency Medicine at Emory University in Georgia, new anti-terrorist centers ". . . are conducting drills on how to respond to weapons of mass destruction, but how many are directing additional resources to meet the threat of large-scale terrorism with explosives?" Injuries that result from explosives

In the midst of an unfamiliar and dangerous situation, whether a natural disaster or a terrorist attack, it is tempting to act according to certain human instincts. It seems perfectly natural to stop to offer help to others...But, especially in the situations we are discussing here, taking time to do so could well put your own survival at risk . . . Your first priority is to survive. Then, given the dangers that radiological dust, radioactive fallout, and chemical agents present to the human body, you must decontaminate yourself. Recognize that you may not be able to help anyone else; most individuals are not qualified to provide the kind of medical treatment that would be needed in cases of the attacks described here.— *Rand Corporation Publication*

can be massive, including bleeding, wounds, burns, fractures and even body part dismemberment.

The effectiveness of first aid techniques on chemical, biological, or nuclear attacks is a new area of research. Indeed, first aid might not be applicable in these situations.

CHILDREN AND FIRST AID

The American Red Cross website www.redcross.org and FEMA www.fema.gov have a great deal of information about children and emergencies. The most important step you can take is to practice emergency scenarios with your children.

Family members as young as 13 years old perform basic first aid and are welcome into first aid and CPR classes. The American Red Cross sponsors a class called First Aid for Children Today (FACT). In addition to learning how to respond to several kinds of injuries, it teaches behaviors to avoid, behaviors that cause injury or illness, such as drug or alcohol use. The American Red Cross also sponsors a First Aid for Babysitters class. Even younger children can perform helpful tasks that lower the risk of injury to your family during a disaster.

YOUR FIRST AID KIT

Dr. Howard Howard, who invented the term "first aider" identifies resourcefulness as an important skill. He describes resourcefulness as " . . . the ability to use to the best advantage possible whatever is at hand to prevent further damage and promote recovery." Having a first aid kit is the best way to be resourceful. Remember, during a disaster the more that is organized, the less you have to think about. Instead of searching for supplies, you can concentrate on making fast decisions and focusing on your family's needs.

Your first aid kit centralizes all necessary first aid supplies in one place. It needs to be well organized so that supplies are easy to see and can be used immediately. Your kit should be lightweight and portable because your injured may be in various locations and you'll need to be able to tote your kit around. The American Red Cross has several excellent first aid kits you can choose from at their online store at www.redcross.org.

Barbara Bing, a certified first aid instructor in Atlanta, suggests you assemble your first aid kit from scratch. "When a family shops for the items for a first aid kit together instead of buying it pre-assembled, they read the boxes, handle the supplies, and really get to know every item they are buying. It helps them remember what they have, what each item is used for, and what each item looks like. And it's way more fun!" Bing notes.

Assembling your kit involves more effort and time than using a store-bought kit. Whatever you decide, do not use your medicine cabinet as your first aid kit. Medicine cabinets are not well organized. Supplies are difficult to see and therefore, difficult to use. Most medicine cabinets do not have complete first aid supplies, and your medicine cabinet is certainly not "totable."

A store-bought first aid kit is not specifically designed for all disaster-related injuries, but it will do for most injuries. Check the list of essential first aid supplies below,

I use the scenario that I have fallen down the stairs. We talk about what the children see, whether that might be blood, pain, or unconsciousness, and what they should do. This includes calling 911 and giving the necessary information, unlocking the front door, meeting the ambulance or the police, or whatever else they can think of to do. Kids do great in an emergency if they are not surprised and fearful of something unexpected.— *Amy Fitzgerald, physician assistant and professional organizer.*

Nanci McGraw appreciates the importance of a surgical mask in a first aid kit. She documented her reactions to the California wildfires as they were occurring by sending e-mails to close friends. "An ash cloud from the wildfires hung over the entire county," she wrote. "The decrease in winds was good for firefighters but bad for breathing. I haven't breathed clean air in days. Sometimes it nauseates me. The whole world smells like an overused ashtray. My stomach thinks my throat has become a chimney. We've been wearing surgical-type masks and they help."

and customize your store-bought kit so that it contains all the supplies listed. In addition to standard first aid supplies, your kit will need specific medications and other items customized to your family's medical needs. Chances are when you add these to a store-bought first aid kit, the contents will no longer fit in the store-bought container, so you'll likely need to buy a new container.

WHAT TO INCLUDE IN YOUR KIT (AND WHY)

When you assemble your own first aid kit, you will require a manual. Manuals can be obtained from any office of the American Red Cross, your local library, and from your state or county emergency management offices. Make sure it is a recent edition; first aid practices do change occasionally. Use a manual with sim-

ple text and easy-to-follow drawings.

Your first aid kit is incomplete unless it is customized to the particular medical needs of your family. Consider adding the following items; as appropriate:

- A 3-5 day supply of prescription medications, important over-the-counter medications, and any vitamins or supplements your family members depend on for their health. Especially important are those that keep a medical condition from worsening like seizures, asthma, cardiovascular disorders, diabetes, psychiatric conditions, HIV, or thyroid disorders.
- Equipment for medications that are injected, pump-delivered or administered with a nebulizer.
- Hearing aids, pacemaker batteries or insulin needles.
- An extra pair of eyeglasses and contact lenses.

CONTENTS OF A FIRST AID KIT

First aid manual with concise text and clear drawings

Sterile adhesive bandages (Band-aids©), multiple size, 10 of each

Butterfly closures (2) to hold wound edges firmly together

Nonstick sterile pads, 2 inch and 4 inch square (6 each) for bleeding, draining, and covering wounds, burns and infections

Adhesive tape, non-allergic, One half inch wide roll for securing gauze and pad dressings

Triangular bandages (3) for arm slings, binders for splints, head dressing and other bandaging needs

Roller bandages, 2 inch and 3 inch, one roll each

Analgesic pain reliever, non-aspirin

First aid cream with an antibiotic to prevent contamination of cleansed wounds

Ice pack (the chemical, non-freezing type) for reducing pain and swelling

Saline eyewash for washing irritants from the eyes

Tweezers (a good, pointy pair) for removing splinters

Mild, anti-bacterial, liquid soap for cleansing wounds and hands

Scissors (small, sharp and pointy)

Tongue depressors for making small splints

Surgical masks to minimize airborne disease transmission and to protect against airborne particulates

Gloves (non-latex, disposable) to prevent blood-borne disease transmission

Moistened towelettes for general cleanliness

CPR-barrier kit. It permits airflow but minimizes the transmission of disease. A barrier kit includes a plastic mouthpiece and a pair of disposal gloves.

Personal Medical Form (see Appendix H)

TIP Shannon Froelich, a parent and Atlanta-based professional organizer, includes lollipops in her first aid kit. Sucking on them has a calming effect on children who are being bandaged or otherwise tended to.

Be aware that items in your first aid kit will expire. For example, eyewash lasts about 30 months, and moistened towelettes last about six months. Read the labels of all the contents of your first aid kit. Stick a label on each item with a specific expiration date for easy replenishment.

Refilling personal medications and prescriptions may be difficult during a disaster. Your local pharmacy may be closed, or their computer system might be down. Try to maintain your regular supply plus enough personal and prescription medications for 72 hours. You can arrange for your doctor or pharmacist to store prescription medications for you. Remember, however, that if your doctor and your pharmacist are in your neighborhood and disaster strikes, their facilities may be as affected as your home and you may find your medications are inaccessible.

PERSONAL MEDICAL FORM

A Personal Medical Form provided in the Appendix, is important to have if you need a prescription filled on an emergency basis during or after a disaster. In addition to summarizing the prescriptions or other medications that each family member needs, it records significant medical histories such as surgeries, hospitalizations, and illnesses. Include the Personal Medical Form in your first aid kit. Make a copy and put it in your essential documents container (see Chapter Three).

MEDICAL RELEASE FORM

In a true, life-or-death emergency, qualified medical personnel will treat your child in your absence. For less dire medical situations, however, you may want to consult with your pediatrician and your children's school or day care center to determine if a Medical Release Form should be filed. Make sure medical alert tags or bracelets are always worn. Be certain the alert tags or bracelets indicate religious restrictions, if applicable. When disaster strikes, it may be too late to find them and put them on.

WHERE TO KEEP YOUR FIRST AID KIT

Hang your first aid kit on the wall or store it on a shelf near your disaster provisions (see Chapter Nine). Keep your first aid kit low enough for easy access but high enough to be inaccessible to small children. Make sure the entire family knows where its kept and don't change its location. If you use it, replenish it and return it to its dedicated location.

TIP Darkness may be an added part of your disaster situation. Put reflective tape on your first aid kit so that it glows in the dark.

DONATE BLOOD

You and your family can help your community, your state, and indeed the whole nation to be more disaster-prepared by donating blood. According to the American Red Cross, every donation of blood has the power to save as many as three lives. How many investments do you have that yield 300 percent rate of return? In America, someone needs a blood transfusion every two seconds due to disasters, accidents, disease or injury, or for premature infants. Donating blood takes about one hour and costs you nothing but your time. Whole blood has a shelf life of only 42 days, give blood and give regularly.

What Kids Can Do

- Learn the parts of the body
- Practice make-believe bandages on dolls and stuffed animals
- Learn what's inside a first aid kit with age-appropriate instruction on what each item is and how it is used
- Help shop for first aid kit supplies
- Take first aid classes

CHAPTER NINE

Hunkering Down

If I Only Knew Then What I Know Now..."*The tornado of 2000 hit at midnight. I got my 14-year-old and 11-year-old kids into the hall of the house. An irrigation pipe came crashing through the ceiling. The house was destroyed, but thank goodness we were okay. Eleven people died that day. In 2003, another tornado came. It followed just about the identical path as the first one. This time we were organized. We had a weather radio, cell phones and a plan. We had supplies to use if we needed to stay in our home. Everybody had a job to do. And we knew how to take shelter in our own home. Gratefully, the wind shifted and our house was missed, but four people died that day.*" — Ann Lamb

Hunkering down means seeking shelter and protection in your home because a disaster has rendered impossible activities outside of your home. Bad weather, man-made disasters such as a chemical spill, or certain kinds of terrorist attacks may make hunkering down in your home the most logical way to protect your family instead of evacuating to a shelter. Your job is to prepare your home in advance so your family can hunker down as safely and comfortably as possible without electricity, water, or gas.

Disaster experts call this hunkering down process "sheltering-in-place." They recommend enough provisions to see you through 72 hours, the equivalent of three days and three nights. The 72 hour tradition is based on historical accounts of major weather-related disasters. On average, it may take 72 hours before emergency crews have stabilized the area enough for you to venture out safely or for them to reach you. It may take a full two weeks for power to be totally restored to a widespread area. If electrical power is out for an extended period of time, emergency food, water, and other necessities will be set in motion by your local emergency management agency; however those first 72 hours may be entirely up to you.

Every type of disaster has specific hunker down steps associated with them. For instance, if the weather predictions are for a wind event such as a hurricane or tornado, board up windows and doors with plywood. Taping the windows will not prevent them from break-ing, but will reduce the risk of flying glass. In the back of the book you will find resources pertaining to each specific type of disaster. This chapter is dedicated to the most important steps to take overall, regardless of the type of disaster.

THE DISASTER "KIT" THAT IS MORE THAN A KIT

Disaster experts all agree that a disaster kit is of paramount importance. They do not agree, however, on what exactly constitutes a disaster kit. When we think of a "kit" we think of a small quantity of items in a container capable of being portable, like the first aid kit. But

Priorities

During the entire course of your hunkering down period, listen to a radio or TV, battery-powered if necessary. Listen for "all-clear" announcements or other information regarding the status of the disaster. Stay in your shelter until local authorities say it's okay to come out. Do not call 911 for updates on the status of the disaster; 911 is for life-threatening emergencies only.

If someone in your home needs medical attention beyond first aid, call 911. Just because you are hunkered down doesn't mean you should tough it out alone. Emergency personnel will put you higher up on their priority list if they know there is a medical emergency. Until they can reach you, administer first aid, and follow the important medical instructions and support you will receive by phone. Use a landline phone if your cell phone is inoperative.

When my elderly mother moved to Florida after my dad died, she learned that Florida has a hurricane season. Her idea of a disaster kit included a bottle of vodka, a can of tuna fish, a can opener, a book, a candle, and matches. She planned to wait out a hurricane by having a drink (or worse), eating a snack, and reading a book by candlelight. "I'm leaving my welfare to fate," she remarked. Gratefully, there was only one major hurricane near Mom, and she accepted the invitation to stay with friends inland who provided for her safety.—*Ronnie Lucas, Professional Organizer, New York*

to hunker down properly, your "kit" needs to include food and water, proper clothing and bedding, essential tools and emergency supplies, as well as your first aid kit and important documentation. It becomes apparent that with all these provisions your disaster kit is more than a portable kit.

Don't leave your family's safety to fate. To hunker down for three days and three nights you will need:

- **A centralized place** to keep bulky provisions like water, food, bedding, and clothing. Of course, you use these items every day, not only during a disaster, so you may already have them on hand without buying anything special. But moving a redundant set these sup-

plies into a centralized place dedicated solely for disaster eliminates the need to hunt them down during the stressful time of a disaster.

- **Decentralized supplies** placed in logical places where they will be needed. An example of this is a gas valve shut-off wrench kept near the gas line itself.

- **A grab & go bag** of essential supplies such as a radio and a lightweight flashlight. Although this chapter is about hunkering down in your home, you may have to leave your home. In that event, a pre-packed grab & go bag of essential supplies kept with your centralized provisions for convenience is important.

SHOPPING LIST OF DISASTER PROVISIONS

Food: 3-day supply of non-perishable food, including baby food and pet food.

Ready-to-eat, low sodium chicken or tuna, canned or in vacuum-sealed envelopes

Ready-to-eat, canned fruit and vegetables

Dry mix mashed potatoes, rice, pasta

Soups (dried, bouillon, or canned, low sodium)

Juices in boxes, cans, or plastic bottles

Powdered milk or soy milk

Sugar, honey, salt, pepper, spices

Peanut butter and jelly

Crackers (low sodium)

High protein energy bars, granola bars, or other food bars

Instant oatmeal, grits, farina, or other hot cereals

Trail mix, nuts, fruit rolls

Cookies

Puddings, fruit cups, and applesauce

Hard candy, lollipops, gum

Instant coffee, cocoa, and tea

Dried fruit of any kind

Water: 3-day supply of bottled water (one gallon per person per day) in stackable, plastic containers with spigots

Plastic water bottles with spigots, 3 gallon or larger

bottled water in 16 oz. bottles, one per each grab & go bag

Clothing and Bedding

One change of clothing inside each grab & go bag

Extra clothing and footwear per person

One blanket or sleeping bag per person

Paper Goods

Disposable diapers, if appropriate

Disposable forks, knives, spoons, cups, plates, napkins, bottle opener

Toilet tissue, paper towels

Cooking and Cleaning

Digital thermometer to check food temperature

Manual can opener

A half-gallon of liquid chlorine bleach to purify drinking water

Plastic bags and ties—the thick, sturdy kind that can be used for garbage or to seal off safe rooms, and even for makeshift ponchos to protect you in bad weather

Various size plastic food storage bags

Disposable gloves, scrubbing pads, hand disinfectant, liquid soap, and moist towelettes

Plastic trashcan, pail, or bucket to make an indoor toilet if required (or a handicap toilet available from a drugstore or health care supply store)

Toiletries (travel size, all of these are for grab & go bag, see below)

Toothbrush and toothpaste

Comb or brush

Razors

Shampoo

Hand Soap

Deodorant

SHOPPING LIST OF DISASTER PROVISIONS (cont.)

Tools and Safety Equipment

Battery-powered NOAA radio

Lightweight battery-powered radio

At least one lantern flashlight

One lightweight flashlight per person

Plenty of batteries

A whistle on a lanyard (one per person)

One small, A-B-C fire extinguishers

Fire extinguishers to put elsewhere in the house

Fire escape ladders

Smoke and heat detectors

Carbon monoxide alarm

Utility knife, small hammer, Phillips screwdriver, flathead screwdriver, pliers

Dual combination gas and water shutoff wrench

Reflective tape and duct tape

Matches in a waterproof container

Extra key to house, car, and bank deposit box

Battery backup (also called a UPS)

Surge protector

Booster cables, road flares, small shovel

UL-approved gasoline container

Tire inflation canister, jack, lug wrench, spare tire

One can dry gas, antifreeze, and motor oil

Ice scraper and sand or salt

Smoke and heat detectors

Sporting Goods or Camping Type Equipment

Small camping stove with fuel

Space blanket

Cyalume chemical light sticks

Backpacks to use as grab & go bags (one per person)

Reflective vest

Propane tank for gas grill (store this outdoors)

Stationary Supplies

Small, lightweight, plastic container for essential document

Small pad and pencil (one per person)

Compact discs

Drugstore or Pharmacy Supplies

Family First Aid kit and prescription medicines or other medical supplies

Medical alert tags or bracelets

Small first aid kit for your vehicle

Other Items

Landline telephone

Board games, toys, stuffed animals, books and magazines

Extra pair of eyeglasses

Travel pet bowl, scooper, and leash for pet emergency kit

It is likely that you have some provisions to use in the event of a disaster. If so, simply make that provision available by centralizing it with other disaster provisions all in one place. The easiest way to purchase disaster provisions you do not have on hand is to shop for them a little at a time whenever you do your regular shopping. "It looks like a whole lot more work than it is," notes Frances Strassman, a professional organizer who has experienced an earthquake in California and a hurricane in Florida. "When I saw the jumbo-jet sitting in the middle of LeJeune Avenue, the main street to Miami's airport, my brain suddenly understood in a flash what "emergency" really meant. I finally asked myself 'What will I do in an emergency . . . what will I need?' Now I live in earthquake country. I have an attractive storage cabinet right by the front door to accommodate my essentials: emergency medicines, extra eyeglasses, cash, shoes, warm clothes, radio, flashlight. Very little effort was required to organize these supplies, but I know what a huge difference having them on hand will make."

A list of disaster provisions appears on pages 94–97. It includes supplies that are needed for a 72 hour hunker down period, as well as every other provision mentioned in this book.

If you don't own a landline telephone, you can purchase one from a thrift store or yard sale. Plug it in and test it thoroughly for both outgoing and incoming calls.

"Reflective tape really comes in handy. You can put a patch of it on all your children's shoes and they'll glow in the dark. Wrap it around a screwdriver handle or anything at all, and it really helps you find things dropped in the dark," notes Bella Jesus. Bella uses reflective tape during the weather-related power outages that are common in her area of Costa Rica.

An NOAA radio broadcasts weather and disaster information direct from the National Oceanic and Atmospheric Administration. Some NOAA radios do not carry local stations. Local programming is key because it will give you instructions by county and community during a disaster. That is why an NOAA and a regular radio are both important to have.

Board games, toys, stuffed animals, books, and magazines will make your 72 hour stay more pleasant because it may be unsafe for children to go outdoors to play and the TV and computer, main sources of entertainment, may be inoperable. Janet Black found a good source of adult entertainment during the 1965 Great Northeastern Blackout. "All the lights were out. We listened to a little transistor radio that said the power was out all over Long Island and New York City. It would be a day or two before the electricity would be restored. We provided ourselves with no-cost entertainment and our twins were born nine months later!"

HOW TO STORE YOUR DISASTER PROVISIONS

Store your hunker down supplies in a centralized location such as a corner of a room, on several shelves, inside a large, walk-in closet, or inside a cabinet. A large, plastic trash container on wheels with a tight-fitting lid will accommodate most of your smaller supplies. Bulkier items such as blankets, clothing, and footwear can go

on a shelf next to the trash container. A large duffel bag and a dedicated shelf will also do nicely.

When you store food be sure to:
- Date each food item with a marker indicating the expiration date
- If there is no expiration date, put a date six months ahead
- Put older foods in the front and newer ones in the back
- Use up first the foods that are approaching expiration
- Replace expired foods promptly

 **Throw out any canned goods that become swollen, dented or rusted. These are indications of bacteria and may kill you.**

ASSEMBLE A GRAB & GO BAG

A grab & go bag contains crucial supplies you need to have with you if you must leave your home. The American Red Cross has pre-packed kits available to use as a grab & go bags obtainable at their offices and through www.redcrossatlanta.org. For convenience, you can purchase and customize a kit for each family member. Or you can assemble grab & go bags from scratch using the list below. Go over the contents of it with everyone in your family so they understand what is inside and its usage. Stow the grab & go bags with your centralized disaster provisions **with each person's name clearly labeled on the bag**.

- Personal travel-size toiletries
- Lightweight flashlight with batteries already inserted
- Extra pair of eyeglasses, if appropriate
- Whistle signaling for help
- Prescription medicine, if appropriate
- One bottle of water
- High-protein, high-calorie energy food bars
- One change of clothes including extra underwear for each child
- Small, soft comfort toy for each child
- Family photograph (one for each child)

GRAB & GO BAG

"Providing a family picture with a love note on the back does wonders for children. I've seen children clutch those pictures for comfort during a disaster," observes Jason Birch, a FEMA volunteer. Also, a family photograph or recent individual photo of family members can be useful as photo identification if police or other authorities ever need to search for a member of your family.

According to Myvesta, a consumer education and credit counseling organization, Americans feel most secure with about $2,400 of cash on hand. That amount of money in your home, however, poses its own risks of theft, destruction by fire, and the temptation to spend it. Remember, we're only talking 72 hours. $300 is probably adequate.

One person in the family must also have the following items in their grab & go bag. It is not necessary for every person to have these items.

Lightweight battery-powered radio

Family first aid kit

Essential documents

Extra set of car, home, and safe deposit box keys

Credit card and cash

DECENTRALIZED DISASTER PROVISIONS

Ann Lamb says, "I don't have a lot of centralized supplies. Instead, everyone in the family has a job to do during a disaster. Each person knows what supplies they need to do their job, and they know where those supplies are." William Waugh concurs. "My home is my kit. I don't think you need all this stuff in one place as long as you know where it is. The point is to know where everything is and to be able to grab it fast. I would argue for more centralized provisions if you have special needs like mobility disabilities or elderly family members or families with very young children." In any event, the following items certainly make sense to decentralize in the exact location where they may be needed.

- One flashlight in each room
- Water and gas valve shut-off wrenches near the water and gas mains for turning them off during a disaster
- Shoes at the foot of each bed

Disasters will not do you the favor of occurring only in daylight or only with the electricity on. You may need to walk through standing water, broken glass or other debris on the floor. If you are barefoot and it's dark, this can be especially dangerous. Put a flashlight and a pair of shoes at the foot of each bed.

POWER OUTAGE

Power outages are common during many types of disasters. During the extraordinary hurricane season of 2004 when four hurricanes made landfall in the southeastern United States, more than a million people were without power across 13 states, some for nearly two weeks. The power company concentrates its first restoration efforts in the areas and on the power lines that restore electricity to the greatest number of people in the shortest time. Emphasis is also placed on vital community services such as hospitals, emergency services, public safety, and water and sewage stations. Because the power company cannot predict when your service will be restored, you may want to plan for family members with serious medical problems to be moved to another location where power service will be more dependable, until power can be restored to your area.

COPING WITH A POWER OUTAGE

Turn off the electrical devices that were running before the outage occurred. This will prevent the power grid from becoming overloaded when the electricity is restored.

Leave one switch in the "on" position to alert you when the electrical power has been restored.

Unplug computers and other voltage-sensitive equipment to protect against power surges when power is restored.

Advise the utility company of downed power lines.

When power is restored, turn lights on first. If the bulbs flicker or dim, do not plug in any other electrical devices until the power stabilizes.

In the event water service is disrupted due to power failure, fill containers with water for drinking unless you have bottled water stocked.

In winter, water pipes are likely to freeze if there is no power. Keep a steady trickle of water flowing from faucets to prevent freezing, or pour a cup of antifreeze into each sink and tub drain, and the toilet.

Stay warm using the heat sources below. If you cannot stay warm, seek shelter elsewhere.

FOOD

Once the word gets out that a storm or other natural disaster is brewing, people will flock to the supermarket. "It's funny when you think about it. People rush out to buy milk and bread, two of the most perishable foods there are!" observes Jeff Jellets. Food and bottled water will disappear from the shelves quickly. Expect very long lines at the checkout counter. You do not want to be on those lines if you can help it. As inconvenient as long lines can be, the bigger problem with eating during a disaster is avoiding food poisoning, which can result from food

If There is a Power Outage:	
FIRST	Use perishable food from the refrigerator
SECOND	Eat foods from the freezer
THIRD	Eat non-perishable foods you have stocked in your 72 hour disaster provisions

that is inadequately refrigerated or improperly cooked.

When in doubt, throw it out! Use a digital kitchen thermometer to check that frozen food temperatures are zero degrees Fahrenheit or below. Refrigerated food should be 40 degrees Fahrenheit or lower before cooking and eating. Fresh food in a refrigerator will stay cool for about four hours. Thawed food can be eaten if it feels as cold as if you had just removed it from your refrigerator. If there is an outage, transfer some food from the refrigerator to the freezer and avoid opening and closing the refrigerator and freezer unnecessarily. (You can add dry ice to your refrigerator to keep the food cooler, longer but be very careful handling dry ice. It can cause freezer burn your skin.)

Discard any food that has been at room temperature for more than two hours or that has an unpleasant odor or is off-color, or texture. If you have any doubts about the safety of food, contact the United States Dairy Association (USDA) or your local Cooperative Extension Program. They're listed in your phone directory.

Chances are by the time you've eaten the food in your refrigerator and all that great food in your freezer the electricity will be on. If it's not, you have your stock of hunker down foods to carry you through. These great hunker down foods taste good, don't require cooking, need very little or no preparation, do not require refrigeration, and can be made with little or no water. They are easy to store, compact, and lightweight.

"Keep in mind that when disaster strikes children lose their appetite,"

I last ate at lunchtime, thinking I'd be home for dinner. At 9:00 at night my dinner was a quart of ice cream from a grocery store. The restaurants were giving the ice cream away since they could no longer keep it cold. I was thirsty. It was 90 degrees. There are no public water fountains in New York City. Finally, the Red Cross arrived with bottles of water. There's no way you can anticipate where you will be when a disaster strikes, but as soon as I can, I'm stashing food and water at home and at the office.—*Cleveland office worker, The Great Blackout of 2003 notes Roslyn Harris, an American Red Cross emergency shelter supervisor. "Children may become sick to their stomachs with either diarrhea or vomiting. Can you imagine a child scared and stressed out and you open a can of tuna?" Harris suggests that a parent pack a few comfort foods. Don't forget a manual can opener! "My neighbors and I shared our manual can opener after the hurricane. It traveled back and forth across the street for five days," laughs Lynda Turner who has experienced hurricanes first-hand in two different states.*

COOKING ALTERNATIVES

If the electrical power goes out, there are other cooking alternatives. "Gas grills are a saving grace. Have an extra, full tank of propane handy. Hibachis and charcoal grills are good, too. Water on a grill takes forever to boil for coffee, but having coffee is well worth the wait," quips Turner.

- A wood, charcoal, or gas burning outside barbecue is a good choice. Never bring a barbecue indoors. Even a wood-burning barbecue has the potential of emitting dangerous carbon monoxide gas into the air.
- Stoves inside campers, trailers, motor homes, or boats are excellent cooking sources because they are powered by generators and not dependent on electricity.
- Outside camp stoves that use gas fuels variously known as butane, Sterno, white gas, or propane are another cooking source. Use them outside to avoid exposure to carbon monoxide.
- A microwave oven powered by a UPS battery-back up is another choice.
- Chafing dishes and fondue pots powered by Sterno will warm but they will not cook.

TIP Before heating any food in a can, remove the label to prevent it from igniting.

MEALS-READY-TO-EAT (MRES)

An MRE is a totally self-contained, full-sized entree with beverage and dessert. Each has about 2,000 calories packed in a flexible, lightweight bag that is easy to transport. MREs were designed to sustain an individual engaged in military activities or during military operations when normal food service is not available. MREs last for years, depending on the conditions in which they are stored. While MREs may be eaten cold, the bag is designed to be warmed in a pan of warm water, in direct sunlight, or on a warm surface (but not by direct heat or flame to the bag itself). You can buy MREs from sporting good stores or on the Internet.

WATER

It's hard to imagine that you can't just turn on your water tap and drink water whenever you want to, but during a power outage, water filtration, aeration, and purification systems can come to halt. The water supply then becomes contaminated with bacteria harmful to your health. The good news is that alternative sources of water are abundantly available. During times of stress (and a power outage counts as a time of stress!) electrolytes in our bodies become depleted and hydration can decrease, which is why water is so important. Limit caffeinated drinks because they increase thirst.

Stock adequate amounts of water and your family will not have to worry about contamination or standing in long lines at the supermarket. Figure on one gallon of water per day, per person, over three days (more for children, nursing mothers, and people who are ill). Do the math now, before disaster strikes. Most of the water you'll need will be used for drinking. Drinking water should

Within minutes of the Great Blackout of 2003, the system that supplies water to the city, county, and 69 surrounding communities of Cleveland, Ohio, was shut down. Millions of gallons of raw sewage were released into Lake Erie and the Cuyahoga River. Like many city water stations, none had backup generators. The presence of harmful bacteria and parasites in the public water supply can cause dysentery, cholera, typhoid or hepatitis.—*Adam Foster, former Water Department employee, Cleveland, Ohio, 2003* never be rationed during a disaster. Allow for even more water during hot weather. The remainder of the water will be needed for washing, bathing, brushing teeth, and other hygienic purposes. Bottled water in stackable plastic containers with spigots are most convenience, but you do have other options.

- You can purchase empty, five-gallon, plastic jugs now and fill and seal them in advance of a disaster.

- Soft drink bottles that have been cleaned will also do. They are small enough to store in many places. Rinse them with one part bleach to ten parts water before use. If you fill jugs or bottles yourself, make sure they are sealed tightly. Label them, put an expiration date six months ahead. Rotate expired water out to other uses every six months.

- Camping stores sell special plastic water tanks bags that easily roll up for storage, and then can be unrolled and filled with water. The water tanks bags contain a spout.

- If you have a large freezer, stored ice can be melted down for later use but this won't provide you with much water.

> **TIP** Don't use milk cartons to store water, as they contain too much bacteria. Never store bottled water in glass bottles because of the risk of breakage.

Your house has a "secret" water source, one that Cyndi Seidler found out about during the Northridge, California, earthquake of 1994. The quake registered 6.7 on the Richter scale and rocked the entire San Fernando Valley, killing 72 people died. Cyndi's house was in the epi-center, but she survived. "My boyfriend showed me how to use the fifty-gallon water heater as a water source. Did you know it has a spigot on it? You just open the spigot and clean water comes out. We used it for drinking water and showed all our neighbors how to use it too," Cyndi reports.

Lead can leach into bathtubs. You can clean out your bathtub with bleach and fill it as a water source for cleaning and flushing but not for drinking. Water dipped from the flush tank of the toilet (but not from the toilet bowl itself) is also safe to drink. If you choose not to use these water sources as drinking water, use this water for cleaning, brushing teeth, washing, and other non-drinking purposes.

CONTAMINATION AND PURIFICATION

Rely on your stockpile of water before turning to de-contamination and purification techniques. Disaster officials will advise you when to purify your water. You will know the water is contaminated if it has a bad odor and a bad taste. Water that comes out of the faucet cloudy or with impurities would also be suspicious.

The simplest way to decontaminate water is to purify it by boiling it.

- Filter out debris by passing it through a clean cloth.
- Boil water for five minutes.
- Aerate it by pouring it back and forth between two containers to improve the taste.
- Let it cool before drinking.

A second, simple decontamination technique is mixing water with liquid chlorine bleach. Make sure the bleach is sodium hypochlorite without scents or soaps or other additives.

- Add the following amounts depending on how cloudy the water is:

Decontamination		
	QUART	GALLON
Clear water	2 drops	8 drops
Cloudy water	4 drops	16 drops

- Let it stand for 30 minutes after adding the bleach. When properly treated, the water will have a slight odor of bleach. Don't dilute the water to the point where the odor is eliminated.

Purification tablets are another method of decontaminating water. They are readily available at hardware stores and sporting goods stores. The tablets pack well, store for a long time, and are easy to use. The drawback is that they can adversely affect people with liver or kidney disease. Since some people may be unaware of these ailments, purification tablets may make them ill.

SANITATION

Keep sanitary all food containers and food preparation areas. Wash food containers with soap and hot water or a diluted bleach solution. Wash your hands with soap and boiled water before preparing or eating food, after toilet use, after handling floodwater, waste or any source of contamination. If you don't have a water supply coming into your toilet, it will flush if you pour about two quarts of water into it. Flush only once or twice a day, observing the rule "if it's yellow, let it mellow; if it's brown, send it down." If you have a sump pump that stops due to lack of electricity, consider connecting it to a battery-powered back-up source instead of a generator.

If power or water supply is unavailable for an extended period, you will need to assemble an indoor or an outdoor emergency toilet.

Assemble an Indoor Emergency Toilet

- Use a trash can, pail, bucket, or handicap toilet with a snug-fitting lid.
- Line the container with heavy plastic trash bags.
- After each use, pour a small amount of chlorine bleach into the container to reduce odors and germs. Stand back. Don't let the bleach splash into your eyes.

- To dispose, wear gloves. Tie the plastic bag. Put it inside of another plastic bag and tie up that bag. Transfer to a larger trash receptacle outside the house, if possible.

Assemble an Outdoor Emergency Toilet

- Dig a hole two feet deep in the far corner of your yard.
- After each use, cover with a layer of dirt, and a layer of powdered bleach or lime.
- When it has filled to one foot from the top, fill it completely with soil and begin a new hole.

CLOTHING

Proper clothing will keep you warm and dry, facilitate physical movement through mud, standing water, ice, or other disaster conditions and protect you against injury. It is not unusual for children to soil their clothes during a disaster because of fear and anxiety, so stock extra underwear for the little ones. In a 72 hour period, the clothes you are wearing plus one complete change of clothes per person should be adequate. Layer on extra clothing to stay warm. Include

TIP Go through your clothes and you are likely to find items that are no longer in style but are in good condition. Don't throw away useful boots or sturdy shoes just because they are out of style. Use them in an emergency. Women should use flat-heeled shoes or sneakers only in an emergency.

the following among your emergency clothes:

- Coat
- Raincoat or water-resistant parka
- Sweater
- Sweatshirts and sweatpants
- Long-sleeve shirt
- Jeans
- T-shirts and undergarments
- Underwear
- Socks
- Sturdy shoes
- Hat, scarf, gloves, if appropriate

BEDDING

Stow at least one blanket or sleeping bag per family member. You might also want to purchase a "space blanket." Made of an inner coating of reflective material—usually Mylar—space blankets have the capacity to reflect radiant heat, like the kind the body gives off, back to the body. It is an exceedingly lightweight source of warmth. The outer layer is also rain and wind resistant.

HEAT SOURCES

The safest way to stay warm is to layer your clothing. During cold weather, bed down in a room with the most sunshine. A space blanket is also helpful in cold weather.

- A built-in propane or natural-gas fireplace is a great source of heat as long as the chimney or flue is working properly. If you do use a gas fireplace, be sure your carbon monoxide detector is operating properly.
- Kerosene heaters must be UL approved. Some have enough output to heat a small house, but they utilize liquid kerosene fuel that is difficult to manage.
- Portable propane heaters are easier to use than kerosene. They must be certified for indoor use.

Do not use wood-burning fireplaces or stoves, gas ovens, or charcoal or propane gas grills to heat the inside of your home. The risk of fire and/or carbon monoxide poisoning is too high.

LIGHT SOURCES

You may be tempted to use candles as the first line of defense during a blackout, but even careful adults can accidentally start a fire. With so many inexpensive, effective flashlights available, using candles is not worth the risk. Many models of flashlights are available including hand-held, and lantern types that can be hung from the ceiling or wall. Alkaline cells are batteries of choice because they have a long shelf life, are easy to replace, and last longest when in use. On average the larger the battery, the longer it lasts (expect size C and D batteries to last longer than AA batteries.) Models with xenon, krypton, or halogen lamps will be the brightest and last the longest.

Rechargeable flashlights are less dependent upon batteries, they can be charged directly from the electrical outlets in your home. They work only as well as the charge to them, however, and if the charge runs down you will not be able to recharge them unless you have a UPS. A hand-cranked model that works up a charge from a small internal generator is also useful but tends not to last very long.

Provide one handheld flashlight per family member. Child-sized models are fun for kids to use, as well as

In 1898, part-time inventor Joshua Cowen showed his friend Conrad Hubert a novelty item he invented. Cowen inserted a small, battery-powered bulb inside a flowerpot. When a button was pushed, the plant lit up. Hubert realized that if he encased the battery and the bulb inside a tube-like case, he could project a beam of light. Thus the "electric hand torch" was born. Hubert's company, Ever Ready, would grow to make millions. But don't feel too badly for his friend, also known as Joshua Lionel Cowen. Cowen went on to make his own fortune with the Lionel electric toy train company.

functional. Two or three models that can be hung from ceilings or walls would also be useful.

Cyalume chemical light sticks can be very useful for illuminating a small area. They are light, non-toxic and non-flammable and can last as long as 12 hours. Simply bend the stick and shake it until it glows. Children find them especially comforting because of their green or orange glow rather than the harsh, shadow-projecting light of a flashlight. Be aware that the light of a cyalume stick is less illuminating than a flashlight. Buy the kind that has a small hook on the end so that they can be either held in hand or hung on a hook.

Gas lamps, lanterns, hurricane lamps, kerosene lamps, and tiki torch lamps should be limited to outdoor use. Generators (sometimes called alternators) use gasoline to run an engine that generates electricity to power selected devices in your home. Portable generators can be deadly if used improperly, emitting carbon monoxide that is impossible to detect without a proper detection device. Use a generator outdoors only, and only if you have experience and under very specific circumstances such as the following:

- You have special medical equipment that must be powered (register this equipment with your utility company so that they can give you priority service during a blackout)
- Your home is in an isolated area where emergency crews cannot reach you
- You operate a farm or dairy

 **Never connect a generator to the electrical system of the house without proper inspection by your power company. Failure to have the electrical system inspected can result in injury or death to utility crews trying to restore service to the area.**

KEYS

If you're like most people, the keys to your house and car are on the key ring you carry with you. Many of us also have infrequently used keys to sheds, filing cabinets, windows, storage areas and other devices; we also have duplicate keys for the house and car. These are often unlabeled and stashed around the house and in hiding places outdoors. During a disaster, finding keys and associating them with the appropriate locks is unnecessary stress. Take the time now to organize your keys. Buy an inexpensive key filer that mounts on the inside of a door or cabinet, and label each key.

SAFE ROOM FOR NATURAL DISASTERS

You may need to hunker down in your home in a "safe room." A safe room offers protection against a natural disaster or a chemical or biological attack. The object of a safe room for natural disasters is to minimize the impact of a structural failure to your house resulting in an injury to you or your family. If the roof or wall collapses, or if debris falls or flies, you'll want to be in the most protected room in the house. That room is usually on the *lowest* level with the most walls between the room and the outside of the house.

Bring your grab & go bag with you to the safe room. Keep your radio on and follow the instructions of emergency authorities. Know which way is east, west, north and south. "We were alerted to head for the 'northeasternmost' part of the house. I had no idea where that was. Now that I know where it is, our safe room is located in that direction," says Jone Scott, a Salvation Army Service Unit Representative in Oklahoma. Wait for the all clear announcement from disaster officials before venturing outside.

SAFE ROOM FOR CHEMICAL AND BIOLOGICAL ATTACKS

A chemical "cloud" of dangerous vapors or aerosols may be intentionally released as an act of terrorism, or it may be unintentionally released as in the case of a derailed train carrying chemicals. Remember that the targets of terrorism are chosen for their potential destruction to masses of people or for their symbolism. The chances of your residential community being explicitly targeted by terrorists are practically nil. However, if you choose to create a safe room choose the highest room above ground level as possible and with the fewest windows. Chemical and biological agents tend to be heavier than air and tend to stay close to the ground. The object of this safe room is to serve as airtight an environment as possible to protect you from the hazards of chemically released gases until you can find clean air.

A biological attack entails the introduction of viruses, germs, or other biological agents into the air or water supply or other environmental conduit to induce harmful or deadly disease. The overarching goal is to get medical aid and minimize further exposure.

The effectiveness of safe rooms is controversial. Tom Ridge, the Secretary of Homeland Security advises, "Stash away the duct tape. Don't use it now: stash it away and that pre-measured plastic sheeting for future—and I emphasize *future* use. You probably won't need it, but in case you do, you'll have it available." But some disaster experts confess that duct tape and plastic sheeting precautions are mostly for psychological reasons, to give people something to do, to help them feel more powerful and in control. "The reality is it is not very effective. Nerve agents and blister agents can go through the plastic," notes George Burke, Assistant to the President of the International Association of Firefighters. The

decision about making a safe room against chemical or biological attacks is up to you.

- Pre-cut heavy-duty plastic sheeting to fit the windows, doors, and vents in the room so you can duct tape them quickly.
- Put a piece of masking tape on each piece of plastic sheeting marking the sheeting locations (i.e., "doorway," "vent," etc.)
- Get household members and pets to the safe room as quickly as possible. If you cannot immediately find a pet, don't try. They will seek their own shelter.
- Close all vents and fireplace dampers.
- Turn off air conditioners, fans, forced heating air, and the ventilation system.
- Close all doors and windows on your way to the safe room.
- Cover your mouth and nose with surgical masks or a handkerchief or towel.
- Stuff towels under the safe room door.
- Plug your landline phone into the telephone jack.

Leave the safe room only when authorities say you can. Open the doors and windows throughout the house and turn on the air conditioner and ventilation system to flush out any airborne chemicals. If you believe you have been exposed, seek medical attention even if you have no symptoms. Symptoms are not immediately evident.

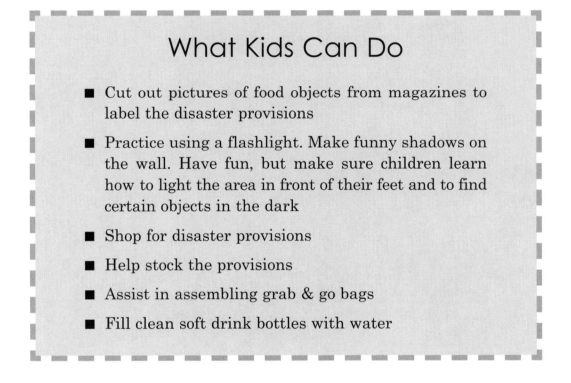

What Kids Can Do

- Cut out pictures of food objects from magazines to label the disaster provisions

- Practice using a flashlight. Make funny shadows on the wall. Have fun, but make sure children learn how to light the area in front of their feet and to find certain objects in the dark

- Shop for disaster provisions

- Help stock the provisions

- Assist in assembling grab & go bags

- Fill clean soft drink bottles with water

CHAPTER TEN

Safely Evacuating and Escaping From Your Home

If I Only Knew Then What I Know Now...*"The wildfires had been raging for days so I began to prepare to evacuate, just in case. We took the opportunity of the waiting time for the official call to evacuate to sort and sift and pitch and ditch our stuff. When the call finally came we had 45 minutes to evacuate. How do you whittle down a lifetime in 45 minutes? I asked myself the question, 'What would we need if we had nothing and had to start all over again?' We were calm. Funny how the mind gets focused in times like these. It was very clear. I call it my 'Do What Matters' List. I put the stuff we wanted to bring with us in small, see-through plastic bags that could slither and shift and fill up the precious space in our car's back seat and trunk."* — Nanci McGraw, professional speaker, survivor of California Wildfires, 2003

PREPARE IN ADVANCE

During some disasters, it is too risky or outright dangerous for you to hunker down in your home. Leaving your home to seek other shelter is called "evacuation." An evacuation may result from transportation or industrial accidents that release harmful substances that are a health hazard to your family. They may be the result of fire or floods or as a precautionary measure during hurricanes. Bomb scares and other acts of terrorism may also necessitate an evacuation. The largest peacetime evacuation occurred during Hurricane Frances, 2004, which required 2.5 million Floridians to evacuate. There are also emergency events that will require you to rapidly escape your home. Chief among them are house fires, gas leaks, and when you are instructed to rapidly escape your home by disaster officials such as in the event of a terrorist attack.

Though you cannot now predict when you will need to evacuate or rapidly escape your home, you can prepare in advance for doing so when the occasion arises you'll be ready. An evacuation checklist and map details where you plan to evacuate to and the routes you can travel to get there. The rapid escape plan indicates the fastest, safest way to get out of your house. Obviously, the occasion of an immediate evacuation or an extreme emergency is not the time to study your evacuation and rapid escape plan. These plans must be devised and practiced beforehand.

There is much you can do beforehand to prepare you for an evacuation beforehand, including:

- Talk openly with your family about evacuations
- Decide in advance where you will evacuate to
- Map out how you will get there
- Agree with your family on what you will take with you given the circumstances
- Plan how to evacuate your pets
- Ready your vehicle

The amount of time available to evacuate depends strictly on the circumstances. A hurricane can provide days of advance warning, a hazardous material spill may provide you with an hour or less, and a bomb scare could require immediate evacuation. Because you don't know what disaster will befall you and how much advance notice you will have, complete the items on the evacuation checklist in the order suggested as time permits.

An Evacuation Checklist form has been provided for you on page 124 and in the Appendix. Complete the checklist with your family and keep it in a plainly marked envelope inside your grab & go bag. Put the evacuation map in the driver's side sunvisor of your vehicle.

THE CALL TO EVACUATE

According to Dr. Waugh, Jr., evacuations have definite patterns. Women with children tend to evacuate first as well as those that are "risk-adverse" like the elderly. Everyone else needs a little convincing unless they have been clearly instructed to evacuate. "Maybe this is due to distrust of the government or because people don't want to leave their homes unless absolutely necessary. That makes sense. What disaster officials now realize is that people will take their evacuation cues from their neighbors. They trust folks who know the situation 'on-the-ground.' Disaster experts have learned that if we get our message out to the community, it will get communicated family by family." These on-the-ground folks are part of your social network. Consult with them during a disaster, and make use of your entire personal intelligence network to help inform your decision (see Chapter Two).

The official call to evacuate will be communicated to you in various ways. Meteorologists on local TV and radio will track a disaster and give evacuation information. The Emergency Alert System will also be utilized. Many communities have disaster sirens or horns as well; loudspeakers or bullhorns are also commonly utilized. When necessary, emergency officials will actually go door-to-door. Learn the evacuation warning systems of your community. Call your local disaster management agency if you are unfamiliar with the methods. There may be times when evacuating makes sense for you and your family even if the official word has not been given. Use common sense. Err on the side of caution. Consult your personal intelligence network.

WHERE TO SEEK SHELTER

Depending on the circumstances, you may only have to evacuate to local friends or relatives. If disaster is geographically widespread, however, out-of-town relatives or friends, or area hotels or motels may be necessary evacuation sites. Public shelters will also be available to you; they already exist in local schools, community centers, and places of worship. In some instances, public shelters are created from tents or prefabricated building materials, especially if they are needed on a wide-scale basis or outside of the affected area. If you have the luxury of an out-of-town vacation home, that can be an ideal shelter.

On September 11, 2001, I was two blocks from the White House in a meeting. My husband, who works two blocks from the Capitol, called to tell me about the World Trade Center attacks in New York City and we should follow our plan. Once the Pentagon was hit there was no way we could reconnect. We knew whoever had the Jeep that day needed to get home to get the dogs and our bags and that we would meet at our cabin in West Virginia. Although I was nervous, I knew we were prepared. I was never so happy to see him pull up to the driveway in West Virginia!—*Carol Schaer*

The fallout shelters of the 1950s were built underground. Many remain, but are no longer clearly marked with signs. Ask your local emergency management agency where the nearest accessible fallout shelter is and mark it on your evacuation map.

WHAT TO BRING TO A SHELTER

What you bring with you to a shelter depends on how much advance notice you have. If you must evacuate immediately with no prior notice put on warm clothing and comfortable shoes and take your grab & go bag. Leave immediately and bring nothing else with you. If you have more time, take items of special value to you already agreed upon in your Evacuation plan. Shelters will have food, water, and bedding so it's not important to pack those.

Marilyn Ryall, a professional organizer, volunteered to help in a public shelter in the wake of a local natural disaster. Her organizing skills were put to good use organizing supplies, sorting meals, and labeling items for fast and easy distribution. She reports that public shelters are quite comfortable but ". . . next time I'll bring pre-moistened cleaning cloths, and a broom and dustpan." The message for you? You'll be safe and dry and warm and fed, however, it won't be as clean as your own house, so be understanding.

When Nanci McGraw evacuated from her home in 2003 because of wildfires, she had time to put on her "coat of many colors", a colorful outer garment so her husband could spot her easily in a crowd. "I also put on my wedding ring and good watch. And my diamond stud earrings. I thought, my ears can carry something."

EVACUATING PETS

With the exception of seeing-eye dogs, pets are not always allowed in a public shelter or at hotels, even well behaved, small dogs and cats. Pets can cause sanitation problems, provoke allergic, and can behave badly under stress just as humans do. Be sure to contact the shelter or hotel you plan to evacuate to in advance and ask about their pet policy. "When Hurricane Floyd hit Florida, many people evacuated over the state line to Georgia. People brought their pet alligators with them, hedgehogs, . . . all kinds of animals. So on top of the usual concerns like providing for food and water and shelter, we had to involve

state Fish and Wildlife officials to figure out how to cope with the animals," complained one shelter employee. If you have enough warning, your out-of-town relatives may be able to put up your pets.

Pre-pack a pet emergency kit in a small nylon bag. Stow the kit inside your pet's portable travel cage. Include:

- a small food and water bowl
- vacuum-packed food
- medications
- collar and leash
- favorite toy
- plastic bags and scooper

VEHICLE READINESS

Your car is likely going to be your evacuation vehicle and you'll want it to be able to drive long distances (or sit in long lines of traffic) safely and with some degree of comfort. Keep your vehicle in good working order at all times.

TIP A tank of gas averages 150 to 200 miles, depending on driving conditions and the efficiency of your vehicle's engine. Plan to evacuate to a shelter within that range to avoid having to find gasoline.

- Perform regular maintenance according to manufacturer's guidelines.
- Make necessary repairs without delay.
- Keep the gas tank full. Gas pumps may not be operating and those that do will have extremely long lines. It's better for the overall performance of your engine to be running on a full tank of gas.
- Check your spare tire regularly to be certain it maintains adequate air pressure
- Prepare a Vehicle Disaster Kit.
- Know how to operate your garage

VEHICLE DISASTER KIT

Vehicle first aid kit (a small, store-bought first aid kit will do fine)

Warm blanket or space blanket

Flashlights and batteries

Fire extinguisher (small, A-B-C type)

Matches and candle in a deep can (to warm hands, heat a drink, or use as an emergency light)

Road maps and compass

Booster cables, road flares, small shovel

Tire inflation device or canister of "instant" tire patch

Jack, lug wrench, spare tire

Can of dry gas, antifreeze and motor oil

Gallon of water for drinking and for the radiator

Several high protein snack bars

Extra pair of footwear

Paper towels

Ice scraper, sand, salt or kitty litter for dissolving ice (unless ice is not an issue in your area)

Reflective vest

UL-approved gasoline container

Cell phone

door's *manual* release lever in case of a power outage.

- Don't travel with extra gasoline. But do have an empty UL- or FA-rated container in your vehicle in the event you have to tote gasoline to your vehicle.

Store-bought vehicle emergency kits are designed for roadside emergencies, not disasters. They are meant to keep you safe if your vehicle is disabled and to enable you to alert help. With a little extra organization, you can make your vehicle prepared not only for roadside emergencies but also for disasters. You can add the following items to a good, store-bought vehicle emergency kit, or you can prepare your own from scratch. Keep your vehicle disaster kit in the trunk of your car inside a duffel bag.

TIP Learn how to operate your car jack and change a flat tire now. This is not a skill that comes easily if you are trying it for the first time on a dark, cold night or under other adverse conditions.

YOUR VEHICLE AS SHELTER

Your vehicle can serve as temporary shelter if you are on the road and cannot reach a safer shelter, or if your home very suddenly becomes unsafe and you simply must seek protection somewhere. With the windows up, the vents closed, and the air conditioner off, your vehicle will protect you from chemicals and dust and ash, and it offers safety from lightning in the event of severe storms.

- Position your vehicle as far to the left of the road as possible because emergency vehicles will need to travel on the right side of the road.
- Put your hazard lights on.
- Tie a scarf or other fabric to the antenna as a disaster flag or spread a large cloth around the vehicle to attract the attention of overhead emergency helicopters or planes.
- Remain with your vehicle and call for assistance on your mobile phone if you have one.
- If it's cold, run the engine for 10 minutes each hour and keep the heater on. Don't trudge off in freezing weather.

- To prevent carbon monoxide poisoning, make sure snow is not blocking the exhaust pipe.
- While the engine is running, open a window slightly for fresh air.
- Keep the doors locked. When help arrives, ask for identification.
- If you exit the vehicle, do so just from the left passenger side.

EVACUATION MAP

Using a current local map, plot a route to where you most prefer to evacuate using a black marker. Include an alternative route to your preferred evacuation site in case the preferred route is closed. Mark this route with a dashed line.

EVACUATION CHECKLIST

❑ Bring the pets to out-of-town friends or relatives or to a local pet shelter

❑ Fill the gas tank

❑ Check that the vehicle disaster kit is ready and packed

❑ Secure your home against wind or water events as best as possible in the time you have available with plywood.

❑ Pack the grab & go bag in the vehicle

❑ Tell a local family member your plans. Call an out-of-town contact with your plans

❑ Pack the evacuation map in the vehicle's driver side sunvisor

❑ Pack the vehicle with stuff you've agreed to take with you (i.e., family heirlooms, computer discs, or heritage photographs)

❑ Write the name and phone number of the shelter on an index card along with the alternative shelter and the pet shelter. Put it inside a zipper food bag and attach it to the front door or leave it in the mailbox.

❑ Turn off the gas in the house (see Chapter Six for more details)

Choose an alternative evacuation site and plot out a route to it in case your preferred evacuation site is closed. Indicate the nearest public shelter and the nearest fallout shelter just in case with a big X. Write out the driving directions and the name, address, phone number, fax, and email address of your evacuation site and attach it to the map. See the sample map below.

IF YOU EVACUATE ON FOOT

Do not walk through moving water. Six inches of moving water can knock you over, causing you to injure yourself or possibly drown. Do not attempt to walk across streams. Be aware of falling rocks and potential landslides and mudslides, and avoid downed power lines.

YOUR RIGHT NOT TO EVACUATE

Even during a federally mandated evacuation, you have the right to not leave your home; however, be aware that if you do not evacuate and you then need emergency assis-

tance, emergency officials are not obligated to respond. The time for accepting assistance has passed and emergency responders will only be put in peril due to your hesitation. If you have voluntarily ignored a mandatory evacuation, you may encounter problems when filing insurance claims or applying for disaster relief. "When a local disaster authority comes knocking on the door asking for the name of next-of-kin, people usually realize the seriousness of the situation and tend to evacuate," offers Jeff Jellets.

WHAT TO DO WHEN YOU RETURN TO YOUR HOME

Don't expect to return to your home immediately. Access to damaged areas may be delayed until dangerous power lines or other hazards are removed, and until search and rescue operations are completed. Report any broken water, gas, or sewer lines to the local utility company. Be very careful to avoid standing in water near electrical lines that may cause electrocution. In the case of floods, insects, snakes and other animals may be more present than usual. Do not stand on the roof as it may have become damaged. Water may be contaminated after a disaster so be certain you know the status of the water supply.

RAPID ESCAPES

A rapid escape may be necessitated because your house is primed for danger. There are three situations when getting out of the house rapidly may be the best way to protect yourself and your family. They are:

- when fire has broken out,
- when there is a gas leak,
- And whenever disaster officials tell you to as in the event of a terrorist attack.

Under these circumstances, it may seem that implementing a plan makes no sense. Why would you take the time to think through a plan and put it into action when all you want to do is run for your life? That's the whole point of a plan—so that you *don't* have to think through any details, so that you'll know what to do in the literal "heat" of the moment. One thing more—you may run for your life,

but it's possible that you may run the wrong way! That's why you need a plan. A simply, *practiced* plan will prevent your family from becoming trapped without sacrificing speed of escape.

HOUSE FIRES

House fires can be started by many kinds of disasters including lightning from severe storms, flying embers from wildfires, gas explosions, or chemical fires. Most household fires are not caused by natural disasters; they are caused by preventable human errors including children playing with matches, space heaters igniting draperies or furniture, falling asleep while smoking, overloaded electrical sockets, and unattended cooking. Whatever the cause, fire is one of the top causes for rapidly escaping your home. Consider this fact. You can expect only about 10 seconds worth of extinguishing agent from a typical home fire extinguisher. That means that if you have any doubt about whether you can extinguish a fire within 10 seconds, get away from it! Survivors of burns often report that they thought they could put out a fire that then turned out to be too big for them.

Help children understand that firefighters are their helpers, and that they are friendly. In house fires, children are frightened when they encounter a firefighter in full gear. The large helmet with face shield, and the rasping sound of an oxygen tank makes a firefighter look like Darth Vader to a little child. Small children often hide under a bed or in a closet when they see a firefighter coming to their rescue. Prepare your children by taking them to your local fire station, where firefighters are more than happy to play with them, offer some fire safety tips, let the children explore the gear and even suit up so that your kids can see what a fully outfitted firefighter looks like. In addition to good preparation, it's a fun family field trip.

GAS LEAKS

Another cause for rapid escape from your home is a gas leak. If the odor of gas is strong, get out of the house immediately. Open windows and doors on your way out only if they open easily. Do not use any kind of phone until you are outdoors as this can set off a spark. Don't turn on a light switch and don't turn on the car ignition. Go to a neighbors and call the gas company. Stay outside your home until the gas company says its safe to return. For more instructions about gas leaks, see Chapter Six.

When that smoke alarm sounds, chances are you will not be able to see. Smoke obliterates all light sources. The heat may be intense. There could be a deafening roar of fire rising and the upsetting noises of bursting glass or falling debris. Under these conditions, and with fear added in, your plan may be for your family to run for their lives, but in the confusion, it is extremely common for people to head off in the wrong direction or be mistakenly led by other family members elsewhere in the house rather than to the outside. Your family could become trapped and die.—*Sheri Lynch, fire prevention educator*

YOUR RAPID ESCAPE MAP

Draw a floor plan for each floor of the house, one level of the house per page. Label each page Floor 1, Floor 2, etc. Keep them simple.

- Indicate the location of each room on each floor, and the doors and windows of each room. Indicate the stairway on each floor. Use the symbols on the Escape Map sample below.

- Using a black thin marker, draw a route out of the house from each room.

- Use broken lines to indicate an alternative escape route if the first is blocked.

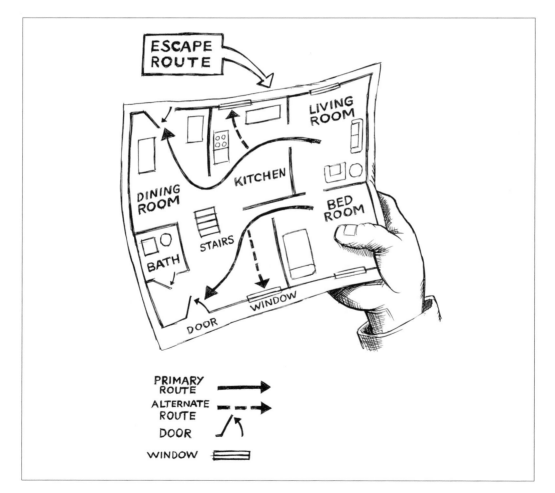

ESCAPING FROM TERRORIST ATTACKS

The likelihood that your house or even your neighborhood will be targeted for terrorist bombing is almost too small to calculate. There is nothing at all different about rapidly escaping your house that would pertain in the event of such a bombing. The only difference would be if the bombing were a "dirty bomb". A dirty bomb uses conventional explosives to disperse radioactive material across a wide area. The detonation of a full-scale nuclear bomb will also emit radiation in a large dust and smoke formation called a fallout cloud. The object of escape from a dirty bomb or a nuclear attack is to put as much distance, as quickly as possible, between you and the source of the radiation. Your defensive escape depends on where the source of the bomb explosion is. Do the following:

- Cover your mouth, nose, and skin

- If the explosion is indoors, go outside immediately

- If the explosion is outdoors, seek shelter indoors, preferably underground

- If underground shelter is unavailable, seek shelter on the upper floors of a multi-story building, sealing the doors and windows and shutting down the ventilation system.

- Decontaminate as much as possible by removing clothing and with vigorously showering or washing.

- Stay in the shelter until you have been notified it is safe to come out.

- When you can get outdoors, escape downwind and as far from the fallout as you can go, as rapidly as possible.

A chemical attack entails the dispersal of chemical vapors, aerosols, liquids, or solids that affect people by inhalation or exposure to skin causing nausea, blurred vision, breathing difficulties, and other symptoms. The overarching goal is to find clean air as quickly as possible. A biological attack entails the introduction of viruses, germs, or other biological agents into the air or water supply or other environmental conduit to induce harmful or deadly disease. The overarching goal is to get medical aid and minimize further exposure. It may take several days to know if you have been exposed or have symptoms.

A Rand Corporation's 2003 publication offers the following specific advice for a chemical attack and biological attacks.

CHEMICAL ATTACK

- If you are outdoors and the attack is outdoors, take shelter in the nearest building and cut off the flow of air by closing windows and doors and shutting off the ventilation system.

- If you are already indoors, stay there, move upstairs to an interior room, and seal it off as best as possible.

- If the attack is indoors, open windows and breathe fresh air. Evacuate the building as soon as possible.

BIOLOGICAL ATTACK

- If health officials inform you that you have been exposed, seek medical attention for evaluation, surveillance, treatment, or quarantine.

- If you are symptomatic, seek medical attention.

- If you are exposed but not symptomatic, monitor yourself for symptoms provided by health experts, and minimize your contact with others.

PRACTICE, PRACTICE, PRACTICE

"Our county is always doing testing and drilling, testing and drilling, so that our emergency personnel know what to do, because we've practiced. Households need to do this too. Little kids 'get it.' They're the ones who come home from school and tell their parents they need to do a fire (rapid escape) drill," Lamb observes. Practicing your evacuation plan and your rapid escape is critically important.

Make a practice run to your shelter of choice and to your alternative shelter in the summer and in the winter to see what the trip is like during all times of the year. Practice your home evacuation and your rapid escape plans it at least once a year, then again whenever the Homeland Security threat level escalates, and during seasons when natural disasters are most at risk for your area of the country. Practice with your eyes closed to become more accustomed to darkness. Practice at night. Include your children. Children need to know what to do on their own in the unfortunate event that you cannot reach them.

It is also important to practice the proper operation of all safety equipment like fire extinguishers and escape ladders. Climbing out an upstairs window and going down a ladder that sways back and forth and bounces out from the wall is a new (and scary) sensation for adults as well as children. Practice getting the ladder out, hooking it over the windowsill, and descending the ladder. It is important to have an adult at the bottom of the ladder during this practice session, to prevent injury. For more information about safety equipment see Chapter Six.

EVACUATING FROM A RESIDENTIAL HIGH-RISE

Apartment buildings and other residential high-rise buildings follow rules and regulations imposed upon them by various agencies like the state Fire Marshal's office. Unlike high-rise commercial and office buildings however, high-rise residential buildings, do not typically conduct fire drills or other evacuation procedures.

TIP Count the number of paces from your bed to the top of the stairs and the number of stairs to the first floor so you won't become disoriented or lost in the dark or under stress.

What To Do Beforehand

- Plan and practice your escape plan together.

- Know the location of the closest exit and a secondary exit.

- *Never* lock fire exits or doorways, halls, or stairways. The fire doors at these exits provide a way out during the fire and slow the spread of fire and smoke. Likewise, never prop stairway or other fire doors open.

- Ask your building manager for the evacuation plans.

- Be sure your building manager posts evacuation plans in high traffic areas, such as lobbies.

- Learn the sound of your building's fire alarm.

- Make sure everyone knows what to do if the fire alarm sounds.

- Know who is responsible for maintaining the building's fire safety equipment and systems. Insist that all fire safety equipment and systems be properly operating at all times. Report any sign of damage or malfunction to the building management.

What To Do When Disaster Strikes

- If your apartment door feels warm to the touch, *do not attempt to open it*. Stay in your apartment. Stuff the cracks around the door with wet towels, rags, bedding, or tape and cover vents to keep smoke out.

- Call 911 to tell them exactly where you are located. Do this even if you can see fire apparatus on the street below. Wait at a window and signal for help with a flashlight or by waving a sheet.

- Open the window at the top and bottom, but do not break it. You may need to close the window if smoke rushes in.

- If you leave your apartment and there is no smoke in the hallway or stairwells, exit according to the building's evacuation plan.

- If you encounter smoke or flames on your way out, immediately return to your apartment.

- Once you are out of the building, *stay out*! Do not go back inside for any reason until disaster officials tell you its safe to do so.

Courtesy of The United States Fire Administration

What Kids Can Do

- Identify a comfort toy or stuffed animals to take in the event of an evacuation.

- Help assemble a pet emergency kit.

- Teens can help ready the vehicle and the vehicle disaster kit.

- Participate in evacuation and rapid escape practice drills.

- Visit a fire station.

CHAPTER ELEVEN

The Essentials

Disaster Preparedness Tasks in Priority Order

- Heed warnings, watches, advisories, evacuation orders, and all other alerts from disaster officials.

- Know the safest way to escape your home rapidly. Practice your rapid escape.

- Install smoke, heat, and carbon monoxide detectors. Install fire extinguishers. Install escape ladders, if appropriate.

- Assemble a grab & go bag for each family member.

- Assemble or purchase a family first aid kit. If you purchase a kit, customize it for your family's particular needs.

- Purchase a landline phone. Purchase a cell phone.

- Complete the family communication plan. Practice the family communication plan.

- Complete a Vital Contact List and put it in your grab & go bag.

- Establish a safe room for natural disasters, and determine if you want a safe room for chemical or biological attacks.

- Determine in advance where you will go when you evacuate.

- Have a plan for evacuating your pets.

- Make sure your vehicle has adequate disaster provisions.

- Practice your evacuation.

- Know how to turn off the gas, electricity, water and other utilities.

- Purchase enough food and water to have on hand for three days and three nights.

- Purchase an adequate supply of flashlights and batteries.

- Purchase a NOAA radio and learn how to operate it. Purchase a battery-operated radio for broadcasts of local stations.

- Take a first-aid course.

- Copy your driver's license, Social Security card, and credit cards. Find your original passport, citizenship or naturalization papers, and family medical records. Put all these documents in your grab & go bag.

- Obtain a bank safe deposit box. In it put marriage certificates, divorce decrees, certified birth certificates, wills, living wills, powers-of-attorney, trust records, stock and bond certificates, property deeds, copies of vehicle registrations, and appraisals of collectibles, jewelry, and other valuables.

- Read your homeowner's policy and change your coverage if necessary.

- Insure your valuables, including jewelry, art, collectibles, and antiques.

- Regularly download essential business information from your home computer to disc. Store the discs in the bank safe deposit box.

- Protect heritage photographs and other heirlooms.

- Donate time to a disaster agency.

- Donate money to a disaster agency.

RESOURCES

to Prepare Your Family and Home for Any Natural or Unnatural Disaster

Bioterrorism
www.bt.cdc.gov
http://bioterrorism.dc.gov/main.shtm

Disabilities (Preparedness for people with disabilities)
www.redcross.org/services/disaster/
    beprepared/disability.pdf

Disaster Preparedness
www.redcross.org
www.fema.gov
www.dhs.gov

Disaster Recovery
www.disaster-recovery-guide.com

Earthquake
http://wwwneic.cr.usgs.gov/

Fire Protection
www.nfpa.org
www.usfa.fema.gov

First Aid
www.redcross.org

Flood
http://www.emd.wa.gov/5-prep/
    trng/pubed/flood2.htm
http://www.bt.cdc.gov/disasters/
    floods/readiness.asp

Food and Water
http://www.fema.gov/library/emfdwtr.
    shtm
http://www.aces.edu/dept/edres/
    preparedness

Hurricane
http://www.nhc.noaa.gov/

Insurance
www.insurance.com
www.insurancefinder.com

Mitigation
www.ibhs.org

Papers/Documents
www.docukeeper.com
http://www.montana.edu/wwwpb/
    pubs/mt9611.html

Pets
www.hsus.org
www.aspcs.rg

Photos
http://genealogy.about.com
www.aic.stanford.edu

Safety Equipment
www.homesafetycouncil.org
www.safetycentral.com

Tornados
www.spc.noaa.gov/faq/tornado/
www.fema.gov/hazards/tornadoes/

Weather
www.cnn.com/weather/
www.weather.com
www.noaa.gov

VITAL CONTACTS (Put in Essential Documents Container)

	Name	Phone	E-mail	Acct. No.
Employer				
Bank				
Investment Institution				
Credit Card Company				
Insurance agent				
Appraiser				
Electric Company				
Gas Company				
Water Company				
Other Utility				

VITAL CODES

	Password	User Code
Internet Service Provider		
Bank		
Pharmacy		
Merchandiser		
Financial account		
ATM		
Security system		
Cell phone lock		

AUTHORIZATION FOR WORK AND
DIRECT PAYMENT FOR EMERGENCY SERVICE

As the principal/agent for all owners of the property known as _____,
                                                                    (address of property)

which is currently adequately insured by _____,
                                              (name of insurance company)

I authorize _____ to commence emergency
                        (name of service company)

services to preserve and protect the property from further loss, as mandated by policy number:

_____ as a result of loss caused by
              (policy number)

_____.
              (fire, smoke, water, wind, hail, vandalism damage)

Brief description of work: _____

_____.

As the principal/agent for all owners of this property, I direct the above insurance company

to pay the service provider within sixty days from today. I further direct that if settled in lump

sum, their name be included on any check or draft issued regarding this claim. I understand

that I am responsible for the deductible.

Date: _____   Signed: _____
                                        (Agent for all owners)

                          Print Name: _____
                                            (Print agent name)

Date: _____   Accepted by: _____
                                          (For service company)

Form 191   Courtesy Disaster Masters Inc.®

HOME INVENTORY

Item Name	Description	Quantity	Brand/ Manufacturer	Serial/ Model No.	Where Purchased or Obtained	Date Of Purch. or Age	Current Value or Repl. Cost

MITIGATION AND HOME HAZARD HUNT CHECKLIST

This checklist includes the most essential home hazards to eliminate and the most important mitigation steps to take to protect your home under disaster conditions.

Fire Hazards
- Is gasoline properly stored in UL- or FM-approved containers?
- Are flammables such as paints, thinners, and cleaners stored away from heat, spark, or flames and in a well-ventilated location?
- Are oily rags stored in metal containers?
- Do your fireplace and gas or wood stoves comply with local codes?
- Is your chimney clean? (Repeat annually)
- Has the furnace been serviced this year? (Repeat annually)
- Is furniture and drapery away from the fireplace and baseboard heaters?

Safety Equipment and Safety Precautions
- Is there a Class A-B-C fire extinguisher on each level of the house?
- Is there a Class A-B-C fire extinguisher in the kitchen, garage, and basement?
- Is there a smoke detector in the attic and in the basement?
- Is there a smoke detector outside the sleeping areas on each level of the house?
- Is there a heat detector in the kitchen and in the garage?
- Is there an escape ladder on the upper floors of the house?
- Is there a lightning protection system?

Utility Hazards
- Do you know where the main electric fuse or circuit breaker box is and how to turn the electricity off?
- Do you know where the water main shut-off valve is and how to use it?
- Do you know where the natural gas shut-off is and how to use it?
- Are the locations of all utilities clearly marked with identification tags?
- Can the gas water heater be elevated 18 inches off the floor?

Outdoor Hazards
- Are dead and dying vegetation and trees clear from around the house?
- Is there a plan to secure all the following items?
  Barbecue grills

  Toys and play sets

  Lawn and deck furniture

  Boats

Dog houses

Pool accessories

Trash cans

Gardening equipment

- Is the roof secured to the house frame, and are all the shingles tight?
- Are the gutters clean?

Electrical Hazards

- Are any cords, plugs or sockets damaged? If so, replace them.
- Are the outlets near the bathroom and kitchen sinks GFCI equipped?
- Are extension cords in use? If so, eliminate them by moving appliances or devices closer to wall outlets.
- Is there more than one heat-producing appliance plugged into an outlet? If so, rearrange the appliances or devices.
- Are any cords running beneath rugs, over nails, near heaters or pipes? If so, rearrange them.
- Are any appliances overheating, shorting out, smoking or sparking? If so, replace them.
- Are the correct wattage light bulbs being used in every lamp?
- Do you know how to operate your garage door's manual release lever in the event the electrical power goes out?

Household Hazards

- Is the house free of excess clutter?
- Are old rags, papers, furniture and other combustibles accumulating? If so, discard them. Are rugs and carpets secured to prevent tripping?
- Is your house number clearly visible in the dark?

Earthquake Hazards

- Are heavy and tall furnishings bolted or secured to the wall studs?
- Are heavy or breakable objects on lower shelves?
- Is the water heater strapped to the wall studs?
- Is the water heater fitted with a flexible gas supply line?

Poison Hazards

- Is a carbon monoxide detector installed on each level of your home?
- Are poisonous cleaning supplies under the sinks protected with "childproof" locks on the doors?

FAMILY COMMUNICATION PLAN

Our Family Reunion Spot Is _____

Out-Of-Town Contact (Name) _____

Phone Number _____

Our Home Phone Number _____

Local Contact (Name) _____

Phone Number _____

Father's Work Number _____ Father's Cell Number _____

Mother's Work Number _____ Mother's Cell Number _____

Other Family or Household Member's Work And Cell Numbers (Name) _____

Work Number _____ Cell Number _____

Nearest Relative (Name) _____

Phone Number _____

Other Relative (Name) _____

Phone Number _____

Nearest Hospital Phone Number _____

Family Doctor (Name) _____ Phone Number _____

School or Day Care (Phone) _____ Address _____

School or Day Care (Phone) _____ Address _____

[affix recent photograph of entire family or of individual family members here]

THE CONTENTS OF A FIRST AID KIT

- First aid manual with concise text and clear drawings
- Sterile adhesive bandages (Band-aids©), multiple size, 10 of each
- Butterfly closures (2)
- Nonstick sterile pads, 2 inch and 4 inch square (6 each)
- Adhesive tape, non-allergic, 1 half inch wide roll
- Triangular bandages (3)
- Roller bandages, 2 inch and 3 inch, one roll each
- Analgesic pain reliever, non-aspirin
- First aid cream with an antibiotic
- Ice pack (the chemical, non-freezing type)
- Saline eyewash
- Tweezers
- Liquid soap
- Scissors, small
- Tongue depressors
- Surgical masks
- Gloves, non-latex, disposable
- Moistened towelettes
- CPR-barrier kit
- Personal Medical Form

PERSONAL MEDICAL FORM

Name	Medication Name	Prescription #	Dosage

Pharmacy name and number _____

Family Doctor name and number _____

EVACUATION CHECKLIST

_____ Bring the pets to out-of-town friends or relatives or to a local pet shelter

_____ Fill the gas tank

_____ Check that the vehicle disaster kit is ready and packed

_____ Secure your home against wind or water events as best as possible in the time you have available (i.e., mount plywood over the windows or strips of heavy duct tape over the windows in large X shapes)

_____ Pack the grab & go bag in the vehicle

_____ Tell a local family member your plans. Call an out-of-town contact with your plans

_____ Pack the evacuation map in the vehicle's driver side sunvisor

_____ Pack the vehicle with stuff you've agreed to take with you (i.e., family heirlooms, computer discs, or heritage photographs)

_____ Write the name and phone number of the shelter on an index card along with the alternative shelter and the pet shelter. Put it inside a zipper food bag and attach it to the front door or leave it in the mailbox.

_____ Turn off the gas in the house (see Chapter Six for more details)

INDEX

ABOUT THE AUTHOR

ANNEMARIE POYO

Judith Kolberg is originally from Levittown, New York, and graduated from the State University of New York at Binghamton in 1975. She founded FileHeads, a professional organizing company, in 1989, and has been a member of the National Association of Professional Organizers (NAPO) since 1990. Kolberg formed the National Study Group on Chronic Disorganization shortly afterwards, and served as its director for seven years. A recipient of the NAPO's prestigious Founders' Award in 1996, Kolberg is the author of *Conquering Chronic Disorganization* (Squall Press) and coauthor with Dr. Kathleen Nadeau of *ADD-Friendly Ways to Organize Your Life* (Brunner-Routledge). The events of September 11, 2001, inspired her interest in disaster preparedness. Kolberg is an experienced consultant, sought-after public speaker, and an accomplished writer on organization/disorganization topics. She is the director of Professional Development for NAPO and resides in Atlanta where she is working on a fictional book.

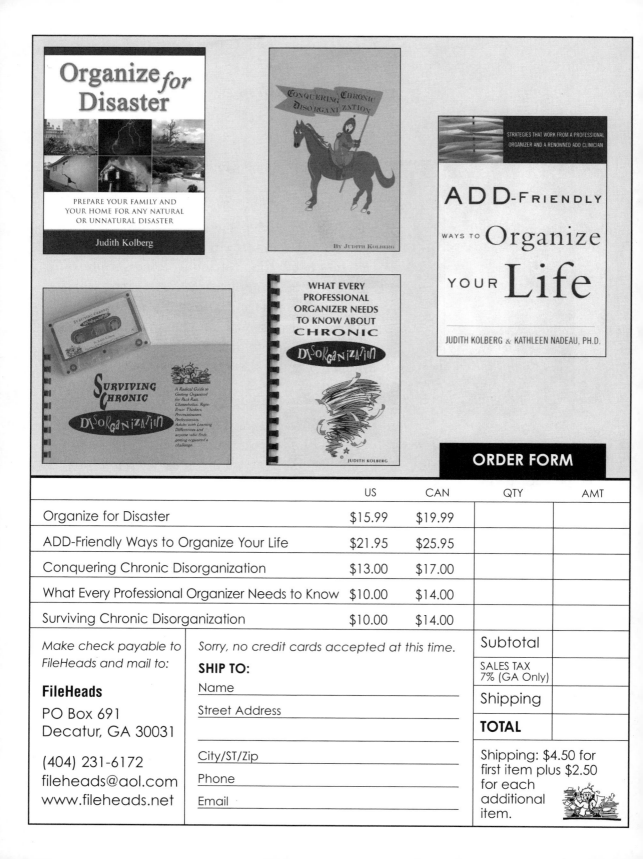

ORDER FORM

	US	CAN	QTY	AMT
Organize for Disaster	$15.99	$19.99		
ADD-Friendly Ways to Organize Your Life	$21.95	$25.95		
Conquering Chronic Disorganization	$13.00	$17.00		
What Every Professional Organizer Needs to Know	$10.00	$14.00		
Surviving Chronic Disorganization	$10.00	$14.00		

Make check payable to FileHeads and mail to:

FileHeads
PO Box 691
Decatur, GA 30031

(404) 231-6172
fileheads@aol.com
www.fileheads.net

Sorry, no credit cards accepted at this time.

SHIP TO:

Name

Street Address

City/ST/Zip

Phone

Email

Subtotal	
SALES TAX 7% (GA Only)	
Shipping	
TOTAL	

Shipping: $4.50 for first item plus $2.50 for each additional item.